The Research Impact Handbook

Mark S. Reed

Fast Track Impact

First published 2016
by Fast Track Impact www.fasttrackimpact.com
St Johns Well, Kinnoir, Huntly, Aberdeenshire AB54 7XT

British Library Cataloguing-in-Publication Data
A catalogue record for this book is available from the British Library

This book should be cited as:
Reed, M.S. (2016). The Research Impact Handbook. Fast Track Impact.

ISBN: 978-0-9935482-0-8 (pbk)
ISBN: 978-0-9935482-1-5 (ebk)

Cover design by: Anna Sutherland

To Hazel, Alfie and Isobel, in the hope that your incurable curiosity is never cured

Contents

Chapter 1
Introduction

"No matter what people tell you, words and ideas can change the world."

Robin Williams

"An idea that is developed and put into action is more important than an idea that exists only as an idea."

Buddha

"Good ideas are not adopted automatically. They must be driven into practice with courageous patience."

Hyman Rickover

Imagine what might be possible, if we could harness the collective knowledge of every researcher in the world to tackle the challenges facing the world today. We could do amazing things.

Researchers are under more pressure today than ever before to demonstrate the economic and social benefits, or 'impact', of their work. But we have been trained how to do research, not how to generate impact. This means many of us feel unprepared and out of our depth when we think about working with people who might be interested in our research. It is hard to know where to start. Putting out a press release doesn't usually do much. Even if the story is taken up widely, knowing how to convert media interviews into real economic and social benefits is a whole different thing.

If you have no idea how your research could make a difference, then this book will help you identify practical things you can do to start on a journey towards impact.

If you know the sorts of impact you would like your research to have, but don't have the confidence, skills or ideas to make it happen, this book will give you the tools to move forward with.

If you are already making a difference and want to take your impact to a new level, this book will help you refine your practice and become more efficient as a researcher, so you've got more time to have an even greater impact.

Rather than feel daunted by the challenge, I want to share with you how straightforward (and fun) it can be to embed impact in your research. The principles and steps I will show you in this book will be just as effective if you're researching medical microbiology or mediaeval monasteries; whether you are a PhD student or a professor. They are based on research I have done with colleagues over the last decade into the way we generate and share knowledge, and they have been tried and tested by researchers I have trained around the world.

For many of these researchers, simply understanding how they can achieve impact from their research is a revelation. They discover a new sense of motivation, knowing that the paper or book they are writing won't just end up on a library shelf gathering dust, but will actually be put into practice or change public perceptions. They feel empowered when they discover the new digital tools that can help them reach out to more people than ever before. For many of the researchers I work with, just discovering how many people are genuinely interested in their work creates a thirst to understand how they can engage with these people more effectively. I think people are often surprised how quickly they can start to realise impacts once they understand a few basic principles and start taking clearly-thought-out, deliberate steps towards impact.

People and relationships are at the core of this book. Engaging with people, building and maintaining relationships takes time and patience. This isn't about clever tricks or 'easy' steps, a time-saving app or revolutionary pill that will achieve impact from our research. However, if you build your impact over time, with care and attention, you will find this a very rewarding process. I am passionate about helping researchers to discover how their research can make a difference, no matter how big or small that difference is. Together, if we as a research community can learn how to generate even modest impacts from our work, I believe we can collectively make the world a better place.

What is stopping you putting new knowledge into practice?

We live in an increasingly networked world in which academic collaborations are growing in size and disciplinary diversity. However, there remain many important barriers that prevent us from putting our knowledge into practice. Putting aside issues of funding, politics and other external barriers for a moment, I believe that the greatest barrier is *us*.

When I train researchers, there are two things that come up time and again. The first is that researchers are trained how to generate and test new ideas, but not how to communicate them or put them into practice. Yet researchers are increasingly expected by governments and other research funders to demonstrate tangible impacts from their work. The second issue is that many researchers are genuinely intimidated by the prospect of doing research *with* rather than *to* or *for* people who are interested in their work. It is hard enough working out who might be interested in our work, let alone having the confidence to actually connect with them.

Of course, it is easier for some of us to generate impact than others. A researcher once told me, pointing at a picture I'd shown him of a sunset over a bog pool, "it's easy for you – you've got a sexy research topic". Well, that was the first time I'd heard that particular adjective used about a peat bog. Although I love bogs, I have to admit that they do have a bit of a public image problem. So, I was pleased that the social media campaign that the image came from was convincing someone. Even if you imagine that people will perceive your research as unintelligible or boring, there is usually someone somewhere who cares about some part of what you do, or there is some way of making it interesting or useful. Sometimes it is a journey you can take in a few simple steps, and sometimes it is one that takes years. However, to date I have yet to meet a researcher who doesn't find the journey incredibly rewarding, no matter how long it takes.

For some researchers, it is the final goal that motivates them – changing policy or practice, licencing their patent, or changing public perceptions. For many, the journey itself ends up being just as rewarding. I know many researchers who grudgingly started engaging with people who were interested in their research, who then discovered that those relationships led to new collaborations and funding. Those projects led to new discoveries, which in turn fuelled the sense of curiosity that first brought them into research. One project I led ended up bringing in as much funding from industry as the original grant, and that enabled us to increase our sample size and do more rigorous research. It eventually led to a whole new body of research that we couldn't have envisaged when we started the work, which has become career-defining for me. Of course, there are researchers who don't believe that we should have to justify our existence by evidencing our impact. And of course, pure, non-applied research has equal value and is vitally important. But whether we like it or not, those who fund research (mainly taxpayers) increasingly want to see tangible impacts from the research they fund.

I think it is easy to forget the privileged position we are in as researchers. We have the latest research insights and evidence at our fingertips and (crucially) we have the knowledge to be able to critically interpret and use what we learn. Yet, without realising it, we hide these insights in impenetrable language, on inaccessible bookshelves, out of reach from those who need our knowledge most. The American women's rights advocate, Margaret Fuller (1810–1850), wrote, "if you have knowledge, let others light their candles from it".

With the advent of open access publishing, research is increasingly available online. However, available research isn't necessarily accessible research. We still have a tendency to use language to erect walls around our candles, so others outside academia or our own discipline can't see the flame, let alone light their own candle from it. We need to take down the walls, one piece of jargon at a time, if we want to communicate our research effectively.

But often that is not enough. We still have to draw people close enough to our work to actually see the insights, appreciate their relevance, and turn those insights into knowledge they can use.

Typically, this means we have to cradle the flame and carry it to people, rather than just hope that people will be drawn to the light. Rather than simply disseminating information, we need to actively engage with those who are looking for new insights, understand their needs and work with them to co-produce new ideas that can actually shed light on real-world issues. Some of the most beautiful candles can be instantly extinguished by a gust of common sense when we take them out into the real world. But if we take this chance, we might just hit on an idea that catches on like wildfire.

A relational approach to impact

My point is that generating new knowledge isn't enough; we have to learn how to share our knowledge if we want it to be used and generate impacts. Making our research available online isn't enough. People need to *learn* about our research, if the data and information we produce is to turn into knowledge that can be applied in the real world. To do this, we need to patiently nurture relationships with those who are interested in and can use our research. This takes humility, because we need to listen and learn if we want to understand who these people are, and what motivates them. Having letters before or after our name does not makes us any better (or worse) than anyone else. We have probably all been in situations where people have given us undue respect as a researcher, and in others where we are instantly mistrusted because we are researchers. If you can be yourself, you can usually cut through such preconceptions in time. It is from that place of equality that you can build the kind of two-way, long-term, trusting relationships that can enable people to learn about and apply your research.

This approach stands in stark contrast to the concept of 'knowledge transfer'. Knowledge transfer treats new knowledge like a 'gift' that can be transmitted unchanged from one person to another. If knowledge is information that people have learned and know about, then people may interpret information in different ways as they learn about it. Knowledge changes as it passes from person to person through social networks, as people adapt it to their own contexts and needs (or in some cases cherry-pick and twist it to their own ends). Even if it were possible to pass the gift of knowledge on unchanged, this approach assumes that the person receiving the gift will appreciate it and be able to use it, despite the giver knowing little or nothing about their needs and preferences. We all know what it is like to be on the receiving end of well-intentioned but ill-informed gifts, which we know we'll never use.

Although there are some situations where it is appropriate to simply communicate research findings to the people who might use them, there are very few situations where some level of dialogue with these people wouldn't improve the flow of knowledge. If nothing else, talking to those who are likely to use the knowledge you are generating can improve how you communicate with them, and enable you to better tailor and target information. The reality is that you will probably want to engage with people who are interested in your research in different ways at different points in the research cycle.

6

For example, you may shape the initial research through intensive dialogue with a few key players, giving way to more extensive communication towards the end of a project, so that your findings reach as wide an audience as possible.

There are many different approaches to generating impact, and Box 1 describes some of the most commonly used approaches and definitions. The key point is that impacts from research are the result of knowledge exchange. If you want your research to have an impact, you need to learn new ways of producing, co-producing and sharing your knowledge.

We now live in a digital age where the rules of public and stakeholder engagement are being rapidly rewritten. Understanding the power of these new tools and how to use them cleverly and responsibly can enable you to engage with groups that would have previously been inaccessible. This isn't about replacing face-to-face contact. If you want to be truly influential as a researcher, the warmth of a handshake and a shared conversation over coffee or in the corridor is just as important as it has always been. But by combining the efficient use of new media with everything we already know about working effectively with stakeholders and the public, we can do much, much more than ever before. Furthermore, contrary to popular belief (at least amongst the researchers I typically train), it is possible to spend *less* not more time at work when you engage with these new approaches to work and communication. Working with people to generate impacts from your research *will* take time and patience. However, the very tools we can harness to help us generate those impacts can actually save us time elsewhere in our day. That means we get time to engage with the outside world without wrecking our work-life balance. You will be surprised at how fast you can achieve some impacts from your research, if you try out some of the things I'm going to suggest.

Box 1: What is impact?

By 'impact', we are talking about beneficial changes that will happen in the real world (beyond the world of researchers) as a result of your research. This can include 'negative impacts' such as evidence that prevents the launch of a harmful product or law. Impacts may occur in the immediate or long-term future, and there can be challenges tracking and attributing impacts, which this book will help you explore.

Impacts occur through processes of knowledge exchange and the co-production of knowledge, where new ideas are developed in relationship with the people who will put those ideas into practice. There are many overlapping terms that are often used to describe this process, including: knowledge management, sharing, co-production, transfer, brokerage, transformation, mobilisation, and translation.

Each of these terms is used in different disciplinary or sectoral contexts to mean slightly different things. Some imply a one-way flow of knowledge from those who generate it to those who use it, whereas others imply different levels of two-way knowledge exchange and joint production of knowledge between those who need to use knowledge and researchers. For simplicity, I will use the term 'knowledge exchange' to include all of these different approaches.

Delivering impacts from research is increasingly important in grant applications and in assessments of research excellence. For example, the US National Science Foundation considers the 'broader impacts' as one of the criteria in their grant distribution, and 'societal impact' is considered in the EU Horizon 2020 research funding programme. Applicants to the Australian Research Council have to provide an 'impact statement' as a part of their proposal. Australia and Germany are currently considering introducing impact into their national research evaluation exercises, Excellence Research Australia and Forschungsrating. The forerunner to these schemes is the UK's Research Excellence Framework, which included an assessment of the significance and reach of impacts in 2014.

Each of these bodies has their own institutional definition of impact. For example, the Higher Education Funding Council for England (HEFCE) defines impact as "an effect on, change or benefit to the economy, society, culture, public policy or services, health, the environment or quality of life, beyond academia". More simply, Research Councils UK defines research impact as "the demonstrable contribution that excellent research makes to society and the economy".

A key aspect of this definition is that impact must be demonstrable. It is not enough just to focus on activities and outputs that *promote* research impact, such as staging a conference or publishing a report. There must be evidence of research impact, for example, that it has been taken up and used by policymakers, and practitioners, and has led to improvements in services or business.

Most researchers and funders tend to focus on instrumental impacts, as these are most tangible. However, a range of other types of impact may also be defined, with some types of impact leading to others:
1. Instrumental impacts (e.g. actual changes in policy or practice)
2. Conceptual impacts (e.g. broad new understanding/ awareness-raising)
3. Capacity-building impacts (e.g. training of students or professionals, CPD etc.)
4. Attitudinal or cultural impacts (e.g. increased willingness in general to engage in new collaborations)
5. Enduring connectivity impacts (e.g. follow-on interactions such as joint proposals, reciprocal visits, shared workshops, lasting relationships)

Some research can lead to harm and damage, which we'll want to know about, so that we can avoid or mitigate the worst effects. It is our responsibility as researchers to anticipate and assess the potential consequences of research and work with stakeholders to design responsible, sustainable and inclusive research (for more information, see resources on 'responsible research and innovation' under 'further reading' at the end of this book).

Evidence-based principles to underpin and fast-track your impact

This book takes an evidence-based, relational approach that enables you to fast track your impact no matter what career stage or discipline you are in. Based on research with researchers, knowledge brokers and stakeholders in different research contexts around the world, my colleagues and I distilled 5 principles to underpin impact in the first section of this book. In the second section, I have linked these principles to five practical steps, so you can deliver significant, far-reaching and lasting impacts from your research (Figure 1).

Principle 1: Design. The first principle is to know the impacts you want to achieve and design impact into your research from the outset. I think most of us are pretty good at coming up with research questions and objectives, but we're not used to setting objectives for our impact. If you have a clear idea of exactly what change you would like to see as a result of your research, you can make a plan to get there, and you're immediately much more likely to achieve impact. The first step, which I'll introduce in Chapter 3, will enable you to start thinking critically about the impacts you would like to see as a result of your research.

Principle 2: Represent. The second principle emphasises the value of systematically representing the needs and priorities of those who might be interested in or use your research. Many of us are fairly sure we already know who is most likely to be interested or might benefit from our research. If not, then we'll typically open our address books and the address books of our colleagues to get some ideas of the sorts of people we might want to engage with. The problem is that most of us only have fairly vague ideas about the sort of people who might be interested in our work outside academia. And we often forget that the address book approach is likely to be highly biased towards certain groups of people and may lead us to overlook important groups of people who would have been interested if we had only identified them at the start. Linked to this principle, the second step, in Chapter 4, will show you how to systematically identify 'stakeholders' and identify public audiences for your research. These include the 'beneficiaries' we typically think of first, as well as groups who may be disadvantaged or negatively affected by our research, and those who may have the power to enable us or block us from completing our research and achieving our impacts.

Principle 3: Engage. The third principle is the most important of all the principles. If you were to boil this whole book down into a single word, it would be 'empathy', and it is encapsulated in this principle. To have an impact, you need to build long-term, two-way, and trusting relationships with those who will use your research, so you can ideally co-generate new knowledge together. This is about having two-way dialogue as equals with the likely users of your research, not lecturing them or doing 'knowledge transfer'. You need to think of ways that you can maintain relationships beyond the typical life-cycle of a PhD project or research project, e.g. by engaging colleagues who will be in the post for the long term, and by continuing to engage between projects via social media, newsletters and offering seminars etc. This approach will pay dividends in the end, whether in terms of future jobs and collaborations, or in terms of getting that crucial letter of support for your next research proposal. However, investing in relationships takes time. So the third step, in Chapter 5, will help you to become significantly more efficient so that you have more time to engage in impact generating activities, whilst also improving your work-life balance.

Principle 4: Early impact. The next principle might seem self-evident, but we need to remember that what we might view as impact might be quite different to the people we want to benefit from our research. In particular, researchers have a habit of thinking of impact over periods of at least three years, whereas many of the people we want to work with will be expecting impacts in weeks and months. Partly this is about managing expectations, but it is also about trying your best to deliver tangible results as soon as possible, that can help keep people engaged with your work. There are a bunch of quick wins that most of us can provide fairly easily, for example, early publication of literature reviews (where possible turning these into more digestible briefing notes) and coordinating research milestones to match the time-horizons of decision-makers. We will explore this in more depth in the fourth step, in Chapter 6.

Principle 5: Reflect & Sustain. Finally, you need to keep track of what works, so you can improve your knowledge exchange, and continue nurturing relationships and generating impacts in the long term. In the second step, you will come up with an impact plan that integrates simple indicators you can use to track whether or not your activities are taking you forwards or backwards along your pathway to impact. The last, fifth step, is about regularly reflecting on your knowledge exchange and impacts with your research team and key stakeholders, so you can learn from your peers and share good practice.

In the third part of the book, I have provided a guide to some of the most important and latest tools and techniques you can use to implement each of these steps (with templates provided in Part 4). I have left some topics outside the scope of this book. Most notable are questions around Intellectual Property and patenting your research. This is a complex area and there are many good books that can give you far more expert advice than I am able to offer. If you think that it may be possible to commercialise your research, it is always wise to seek expert advice from within your institution before you speak to businesses. I have also not covered the full range of approaches and technologies for communication, including for example, writing press releases, podcasting, delivering presentations and writing for non-specialist audiences. There are many books, websites and courses that can help you in all of these areas. Instead, I have focused on social media for researchers, where there is currently very limited guidance, but huge potential for generating impact.

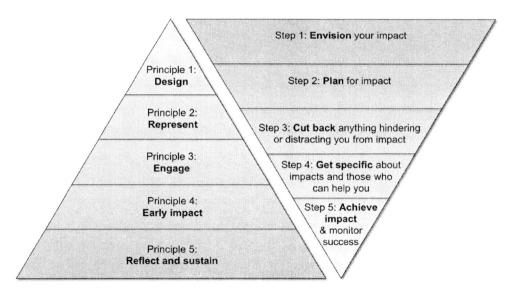

Figure 1: Principles to underpin impact and steps to fast track impact.

Start planting your ideas

This isn't a book of theory. It isn't something to bear in mind for the future. It is intended to be used by you today in the research you are designing, conducting or writing up now. So before you move to the next chapter, choose a research project that you would like to have more of an impact. If possible, choose a project that you're leading or a part of a project over which you have control or influence.

I've written this book because I want to change the way researchers generate and share knowledge, so that their ideas can change the world. I hope this book gives you the tools to enable you to achieve this.

You can plant a seed and it becomes a flower.
You can share an idea and it becomes another's.
An idea really can change the world.

Will you be that change?

Part 1: Principles to underpin your impact

Chapter 2
The impact philosophy: five principles to underpin your impact

Summary

This chapter introduces five evidence-based principles that underpin successful knowledge exchange and impact. Based on the experiences and views of researchers who have worked with stakeholders and members of the public in projects around the world, the chapter provides many practical suggestions for ways you can increase your impact, whilst providing a conceptual framework for the rest of the book. If you want to have an impact, you need to embed knowledge exchange in your research. There are five action-oriented principles that can help you do this: design impact into your research from the outset; represent all relevant interests in your work; engage with those who are interested in your work to build long-term, two-way trusting relationships; achieve early impacts to build credibility and motivate engagement; and reflect on your knowledge exchange practice so you can sustain impacts for the long term.

I still remember vividly the day that the idea occurred to me. If I took the time to explain the idea, you probably wouldn't be that impressed, as it is so obvious. But it is the only time I can claim to have had anything close to a 'eureka' moment.

I remember standing on the stairwell in the echoing old chemistry building at the University of Leeds where I was preparing a lecture as a PhD student. I could try and make it sound romantic but the reality was that I was on the way to the toilet and I could smell the toilets from where I stood, staring at the wall as I thought. Like most good ideas, it was very simple — I just had the good fortune of being the first person to stumble across it. Probably lots of other people had

17

thought it already, but being an academic, I got to be the first person to write it down. I was editing the proofs of a paper later that week and slipped the idea into the introduction and waited to see what happened. The paper was published in *Science of the Total Environment* in 2003 and led to an article in The Guardian newspaper, suggesting that the restoration of peat bogs could be financed via carbon markets. This led to a call from an NGO who wanted to use my idea in their work, and I had to tell them that it really was just an idea, and that it would be at least 10 years before it could actually be used. But if they were up for it, I told them that I'd be happy to work with them to see if we could turn the idea into reality.

A full 12 years later, the UK government launched the policy instrument that had started life in that smelly stairwell in Leeds. I say 'launched' like there was a big fanfare or something. The reality was that we were given a microphone and a box to stand on during a drinks reception and half the audience spoke over the announcement. But it was official, and as a result of a huge number of people's work, building on that germ of an idea, we are now working with business, NGOs, government and landowners to save some of the UK's most beautiful and yet undervalued landscapes.

Ever since my PhD, working with cattle herders in the Kalahari desert, I've been interested in how people can work together more effectively to tackle shared goals. And so increasingly, alongside my environmental research, I have been researching how people co-produce and share new ideas. I've been trying to understand how we can combine insights from research with the lived experience of local people and politicians to make better decisions.

During this work, I've seen first-hand the thirst for new ideas among tribespeople who have lost their grazing lands to thorn bushes and their cattle to drought. I've felt the embarrassment of discovering I was a government 'go to person' on a subject I thought I knew little about (turned out I knew more than them and I was the only researcher they could approach who could explain the evidence to them in policy-friendly terms). And like most researchers, I've had acute bouts of 'imposter syndrome' when I've been asked for my opinion as an 'expert' (the worst were the times I had to present research to United Nations conferences, with the rows of people at desks labelled with their country names — I'm still not 100% convinced that was actually me).

But what have the privileged few (who get these opportunities) got that the rest haven't got? I am living proof that you don't need to be any more intelligent, lucky or good-looking than anyone else. I suffer from the same sorts of insecurities as every other hard-working researcher I know, and I've struggled all my life with self-confidence (I actually had a panic attack halfway through my first lecture). However, through the research I have done, and my lived experience of implementing the findings of my research, I believe that there are a small number of key principles that can enable anyone to significantly increase the impact of their research.

In this chapter, I'm going to introduce you to these principles. In the subsequent chapters, a series of steps will be built upon these principles. Each of the tools and approaches in the second part of this book are also based on these principles.

Five principles to underpin your impact: tips from researchers and the people they've worked with

I often hear great ideas and case studies about engaging with people who might be interested in or want to use our research. Those ideas have ranged from the obvious (I can't believe I didn't think of doing that already), to innovative, unusual ideas (that I'd love more people to hear about). Recently, I decided it was time to look at these ideas more systematically. I wanted to find out what researchers around the world were doing, so that the research community as a whole could start to learn from what works.

As a researcher, I know that many of you will want to read the original research, but I'm not going to bore you with the details here (you can pop over to my personal website to read the papers if you're suffering from insomnia). However, it is worth saying that they are derived from interviews with researchers and knowledge brokers around the world, and the stakeholders and members of the public that they worked with to produce (or in some cases co-produce) research outcomes. Working with my colleagues, Dr Ana Attlee, Professor Lindsay Stringer and Professor Ioan Fazey, we were funded by the UK Research Councils to convene a group of international experts in the study and practice of research impact (named in the acknowledgements), to distil principles that could be used to train researchers from every academic discipline. You can see a full list of the original research publications that this book is based on under Further Reading in Part 4, as well as a list of some of my favourite books and articles on the topics covered in this book, which have inspired my thinking.

Figure 2 shows what emerged from our interviews with researchers and stakeholders. The themes around the outside give you a flavour of what emerged from the interviews, and you can see how we've grouped them under five principles of effective impact: design, represent, engage, impact, and reflect and sustain (Figure 3). There is some overlap between the principles and they are not meant to be implemented in any particular order, even though some principles will underpin the application of others. Table 1 captures some of the ideas people told us about. These suggestions are adapted from quotes, based on a qualitative analysis of what researchers and stakeholders told us worked most effectively in their work. Hopefully those tips give you a flavour of the principles that follow.

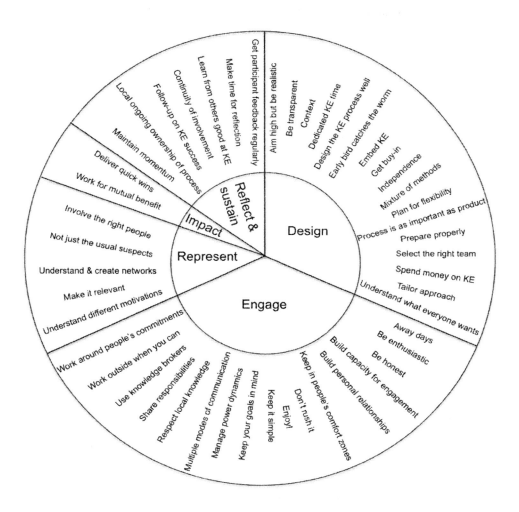

Figure 2: Themes relating to effective knowledge exchange (KE) and research impact that emerged from an analysis of interview transcripts by Reed et al. (2014), showing how these themes map onto five principles of effective impact

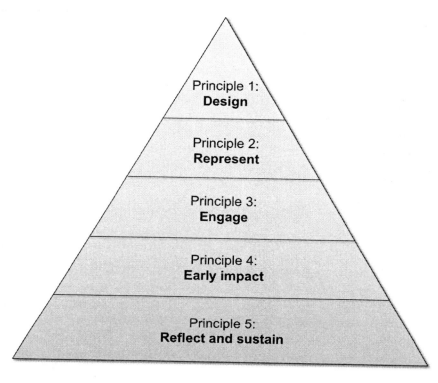

Figure 3: Principles to underpin impact

In the following chapters in Part 1 of the book, I'm going to unpack each of these principles briefly in turn, so that we've got a firm foundation upon which to start taking action and generating impact. In each of these chapters, I will illustrate each principle with practical suggestions about how you can apply them in your research. Part 2 of the book then builds on these principles to walk you through five steps to fast-track your impact. Parts 3 and 4 then provide more detailed guidance on specific tools and templates you can use to facilitate impact in your research.

Design

Understand what everyone wants. Spend time understanding what different stakeholders and project members want from the research. This can help in managing expectations and identifying potential issues/problems early on. It is important that all involved know the objectives of the project and what their role is likely to be as well as the project outputs and any recognition they may gain from their involvement. Time spent at the beginning introducing each other and sharing personal motivations and goals is helpful.

Understand the context of the project. Understand local characteristics, traditions, norms and past experiences, and use this as a starting point for planning the project. Some projects have found it useful to carry out ethnographic research prior to starting their research to ensure their plans match the needs and preferences of local communities.

Take your time. Knowledge exchange is time-consuming if done properly. If not done properly, bridges can be burnt that will influence not only the effectiveness of the present project but projects to come. Plan for the time it will take to do knowledge exchange properly, including skilled staff time.

Design your knowledge exchange activities carefully. It is vital to plan the knowledge exchange process well. Spend time researching the context, the stakeholders and possible approaches. Look into alternative approaches, so you have a Plan B. Design for flexibility, get feedback and adapt your plans, and always try and adapt your plans to suit changing circumstances. It is best to plan to use a range of methods and approaches in the design of your knowledge exchange activities.

The early bird catches the worm. Knowledge exchange activities should be initiated early in the project. Ideally, planning and research into the context and stakeholders should begin prior to project commencement.

Get buy-in. Ownership and ongoing commitment to your research can be quickly established by getting 'buy in' from the key stakeholders. This can be formal (e.g. in the form of monetary investment or contracted time to the project) or informal (e.g. regular engagement via social media).

Independence. Ensure that the management of the research is seen as independent and neutral, so you can build trust with stakeholders. This can be achieved through a neutral organisation leading the process or an independent facilitator running sessions with stakeholders.

Mix up your methods. Plan to use a variety of methods for engaging with stakeholders and the public. Different people will enjoy and be best suited to different methods. Always start with those methods that will be the most comfortable for people, and as trust builds, more innovative methods can be used.

The process is as important as the outcome. How a knowledge exchange process is implemented is often as important as the final impact. Ensure proper attention is paid to creating an effective knowledge exchange process while keeping impact goals in sight.

Resource your impact. Generating impact takes significant time and resources. There are methods available for low budgets that are reliant on the team's personal time and energy. However, if budgets are too low, corners may be cut and outcomes may be compromised. Budget for a well-designed process, which includes social events, staff time, professional facilitation, refreshments and (in some cases) financial compensation to cover time and expenses incurred by those participating in your research.

Use knowledge brokers. Take time to identify individuals who play a significant role in your stakeholder community and who may be able to act as a champion for your work. Such individuals will be well known by many diverse groups, and able to understand their different perspectives. If you can build a strong relationship with someone like this, they can help you build trust with new groups by proxy.

Present your research visually and orally as well as in words. Aim to present information using sight and sound rather than in words where possible e.g. maps, illustrations, cartoons, drawings, photos, models and readings.

Represent

Involve the right people. Spend time researching which stakeholders are best to involve in your research. Make sure power dynamics between individuals are considered and attention is paid to selecting individuals who have the power to make a difference. Involve all parties as early as possible, preferably in the planning process. Time spent in one-to-one discussions to win over those who doubt the value of the process before you start is well worthwhile. If there are people or groups who cannot be convinced at the outset, keep them informed and give them the option of joining in later. Where possible, work individually with people who are particularly disruptive, to avoid disrupting group events.

Not just the usual suspects. Those of different ages, gender, backgrounds and cultures bring different knowledge, concerns and perspectives to the table. By representing the full diversity of interest in a well-designed process, a project can have a far greater long-term reach and sustainability.

Understand and create networks. Understand the social networks that the people you want to work with are part of. Spend time creating connections, both vertically and horizontally, within and between organisations relevant to your research, to ensure you have access to people with decision-making power and a resilient network of people engaged in your work.

Personal initiative. Many impacts from research are based on one individual's initiative, perseverance and hard work. To achieve impact, you need at least one individual who is willing to push the process through and maintain momentum.

Engage

Away days. Put time aside at the start of the project for the research team and key stakeholders to get to know one another's expertise, background and languages. Include time for socializing.

Be enthusiastic. Enthusiasm for your research and the process of engaging in your work is often infectious. Enthusiasm can help maintain momentum and achieve long-term involvement of participants, even when outcomes are delayed or mistakes are made.

Find out what motivates people. People are motivated to become involved in research for a number of reasons, for instance: academic interest, to learn, fear of missing out, financial gain, professional duty, personal promotion, and to support or promote causes they care about. It is important to take steps to make personal agendas explicit, perhaps through anonymous ballot at the start of the project or explicit discussion. If you are unlikely to be able to deliver what people want, make this clear from the outset. Be honest with participants about what they will gain through participation. Do not have a hidden agenda.

Build capacity for engagement. Create a shared skill base in your team for impact, and include basic training activities in the project early on to improve knowledge exchange and co-production.

Build personal relationships. Impact is all about relationships. Taking time to socialise is just as important early on in a process as time spent on knowledge exchange activities. Schedule in social time in the project and get to know participants on a one-to-one basis.

Build trust. A lack of trust can significantly hinder attempts to generate impact. Spend time explicitly considering levels of trust in the project and how to improve trust between team members and stakeholders.

Multiple modes of two-way communication. Whether face-to-face or via social media, use the widest possible spectrum of communication media available to you, so that everyone who is interested in your research can engage with you via their preferred mode.

Keep in people's comfort zones. Be aware of what is comfortable for those involved and keep within their comfort zone. Have meetings in the local area and in a non-threatening, neutral environment. Choose activities (at least initially) that people are comfortable with.

Enjoy! Make sure the process is enjoyable and interesting for yourself, your research team and everyone else involved. Where possible, make sure the activities you design are really enjoyable.

Keep it simple. Do not assume certain levels of literacy or education. Keep language and approaches simple and accessible. Spend time discussing and agreeing terms to be used, and the best approach to take. A stakeholder steering group may help in ensuring the language and approach is suitable.

Work around people's commitments. Keep people involved by respecting and working around people's commitments. Consult with those you want to work with as soon as possible to match your process to their commitments. For example, it might work best to have morning meetings rather than evening meetings and certain times of year may not work well for the attendance of certain groups.

Manage power dynamics. Power dynamics can have a significant impact on your work with stakeholders and the public. It is incredibly important to recognise that power dynamics play a role in the process and to plan for and manage this appropriately. For example, ensuring a first-name basis can go some way towards balancing power but it is still important to recognise that others will be conscious of who holds a formal role in a hierarchy and will be adapting their behaviour and communication as a result.

Record. In order to ensure transparent, trustworthy processes, make sure that your process is properly recorded. This is also important in order to identify and learn from methods that have been particularly successful or unsuccessful. However, do be aware of methods of documentation, some participants may be uncomfortable with audio or video recording.

Keep your goals in mind. Reiterate research and impact goals throughout the process and keep to deadlines.

Respect cultural context. Make sure that your approach is suitable for the cultural context in which you are working. Consider local attitudes to gender, informal livelihoods, social groupings, speaking out in public and so on.

Respect local knowledge. All participants will have significant knowledge of their community and will be capable of analysing and assessing their personal situation, often better than trained professionals. Respect local perceptions, choices, and abilities and involve all types of knowledge when setting goals and planning for impact.

Share responsibilities. Share out responsibilities and credit in order to help build relationships, trust in the process and foster ownership for those involved.

Early impacts

Deliver quick wins. Ensure that if the project aims to create practical outcomes it delivers on these. Delivery of practical outcomes is a key motivator for involvement, and identifying 'quick wins' for delivery early on can help build trust and relationships, keeping people engaged so you can deliver longer-term impacts.

Work for mutual benefit. Work hard to ensure that the project is of mutual benefit. Spend time finding out what people want from the process and try hard to deliver this. Unbalanced processes, for example, those which appear to be all about academic benefit, can fail to get the best from those involved and can affect trust and commitment to the process.

Reflect and sustain

Get participant feedback regularly. Ensure that you get feedback throughout your research on how your activities are being perceived and participants' concerns/ideas. Such feedback will help the project to adapt techniques and deal with problems as they arrive to the improve effectiveness of impact.

Make time for reflection. Build in time for all involved in impact generation activities to reflect on the process and outcomes. This is especially important when working in areas of conflict to ensure optimum learning and behaviour change.

Learn from others who have achieved impact. Spend time exploring similar work and institutes within your area. Go and visit other projects that successfully delivered impact and speak to people who have carried out similar work to what you are planning. It may be useful to engage a mentor from a project you admire and ask them give feedback on your process as you go along.

Continuity of involvement. Continuity of people involved is important, especially for projects dealing with some form of controversy. By including the same group of individuals, critical relationships and trust develop, which facilitates impact.
Maintain momentum. Regularly monitor progress to ensure that initiatives are built on and objectives achieved or altered as required. Impact takes time and often takes unpredictable turns. If there has to be a break, start from where you left off and build this into the process. It may be useful to call a break for a period of reflection and present it as part of the process. Review sessions, feedback forms and good facilitation can ensure that momentum is maintained.

Chapter 3
Principle 1: Design

■■■

Summary

Know the impacts you want to achieve and design impact into your research from the start:
- *Set impact and knowledge exchange goals from the outset*
- *Make a detailed impact plan*
- *Build in flexibility to your plans so they can respond to changing user needs and priorities*
- *Find skilled people (and where possible financial resources) to support your impact*

■■■

Set goals and plan for impact

I think we are all pretty good at coming up with research questions and setting objectives for the new knowledge and insights we want to derive from our research. However, most of us have little experience of developing impact goals or identifying objectives relating to the knowledge exchange activities we will use to achieve those impacts. Whether you're at the start of your PhD project or initiating a multi-million dollar research consortium, now is the time to set goals for your impact. Even if you are halfway through your project, it is never too late to make a plan. Although you won't be able to do all the things you would have been able to do if you'd planned for impact from the beginning, it is often surprising how many opportunities there still are to change your approach to the project so that you can extract as much impact as possible from your work.

Many research funders now ask us to identify these goals as part of the application process. However, it is surprising how few researchers revisit that part of their application when they get their funding and initiate the research. Just because you got the funding doesn't necessarily mean that your plans for impact were particularly good. Your plans may have passed a quality threshold, but the bar is sometimes set quite low. So, it is always worth revisiting your plans to make them more detailed and actionable. You will need to start planning now for the activities that you will need to undertake alongside your research, if you are to have a chance of realising your impacts. You need a plan. In Chapter 4, I'll help you create your own impact plan, but first, lets explore the principle of planning for impact.

Collaborative planning for impact

The best impact plans are collaborative. You can only get so far planning impact with your research team. Unless you are really embedded within the groups of people who will use your research, it will be difficult to really understand what motivates them, and what their needs and priorities are. If you can develop your impact plan in collaboration with these people, then you are far more likely to engender a sense of shared ownership over the work. When people feel invested in your research, and know that they will benefit tangibly from your success, they are far more likely to stick with you when things are taking longer than expected. They are far more likely to be forgiving when things don't go according to plan. And they are far more likely to help you achieve your impact. Apart from giving you their time, many organisations will actually give you access to resources and staff, which can significantly enhance your capacity for impact. From your perspective, you have willing and enthusiastic partners who can significantly increase the chances that your research will have impact. From their perspective, they're getting access to top researchers and the credibility of your university brand at a much lower cost than they would have to spend paying consultants to help them with the same tasks. We asked stakeholders what motivated them to work with researchers, and the findings may be useful to bear in mind if you want to tap into the motives of the people who are most likely to use your work (Box 2).

Developing an impact plan in collaboration with the people who are interested in your research doesn't come without risks. You need to be careful to avoid raising false expectations, as you will not have the time, resources or expertise to do everything that people suggest. If you've done your stakeholder analysis right (see the next principle and Chapters 8 and 13), then you shouldn't discover yourself in a room full of doctors if you're researching archaeology.

However, you may need to extend your research to include some of the things people want to see. In my experience, stakeholders will very rarely tell you they think you shouldn't be asking certain research questions, but they may ask you to extend your research to consider additional things you hadn't previously considered. Not everything will be possible, but it is often surprising what can be achieved with some lateral thinking and collaboration. If it truly is unachievable within the context of your project, then see if there is someone else who you could put people in touch with, or if there is funding you could apply for, that could enable you to do what they would like to see.

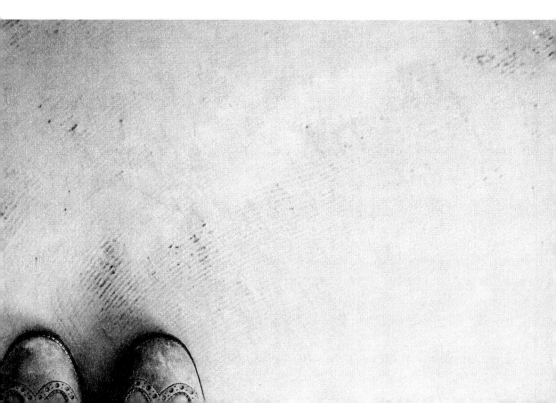

The extent to which you plan for engagement with stakeholders and the public will differ from project to project, depending on how applied or close to impact it is, or how easy it is to communicate with public audiences. For projects that are not yet very applied, where you know there will need to be significant investment of time and resources to transform the work into something that is interesting or useful, it is appropriate to plan for less engagement at the outset. It is not reasonable to expect someone to spend a significant amount of time working with you throughout a project for which there is not likely to be any tangible benefit to them. But even if you think there's another 10 years of research and development ahead of you, it is always worth engaging early with the potential users of your research. Although the company or organisation may not exist by the time you're actually ready to achieve your impact, they may be able to connect you to others who can help you and identify alternative or interim uses for your work that you wouldn't have thought of yourself.

Depending on the nature of your work, it is always worth taking advice to ensure you protect your Intellectual Property before talking to potential commercial partners. However, rather than letting the fear of being ripped off stop you talking to people, try and work out how you can reach out to potential users and start talking about your ideas safely, so you can make the connections (both socially and intellectually) that you will need to keep moving forwards towards your impact.

Plan the timing of your engagement

For projects that are likely to yield useful or interesting results in the near future (even if not during the lifetime of the project), it is important to offer as many opportunities as possible for stakeholder and public engagement throughout the research cycle. Where possible (e.g. using 'seed-corn' funding sources), engage these groups during proposal development and research planning. It is always possible to spot funding applications that have been developed in this way. They have powerful letters of support (that are actually written by the person who signs them, rather than the research team) and their plans for impact are detailed and credible, with named contacts who clearly already trust the research team. In many fields, it is also possible to engage these groups in data collection, analysis and/or interpretation of results, for example, prioritising, ranking and evaluating your findings. For research on contentious issues, co-production of research in this sort of way can have advantages and drawbacks. On one hand, if done effectively, co-production of research that engages stakeholders from opposing sides of a conflict can act as a powerful means of achieving a form of consensus that no amount of additional evidence on its own could have achieved. It becomes hard for groups who don't like the findings to criticise the research when they were involved in its design and execution. On the other hand, if you fail to reach consensus or do not involve certain powerful groups, the legitimacy of your research may be undermined by claims of bias (based purely on the people who were involved in the research).

If you have engaged with key groups throughout the research cycle, then it becomes easy to work together to communicate findings at the end of the project. Each of the organisations you have worked with is likely to want to put out its own press release, and will want to promote the research through their networks. The challenge at this point becomes coordinating dissemination activities (but your press office will usually be happy to do this for you). For more specialist communication to specific groups or key decision-makers, it can be invaluable to work with stakeholders to design your communication.

Working together, you are likely to be able to find the key words and framings that are most likely to make the messages from your research resonate with the right people. And where necessary, these organisations may be able to take your message to these people, whether by opening doors, accompanying you or actually being the messenger. This can be important for communicating findings to key decision-makers who would otherwise be out of your reach, for example, a government minister.

Box 2: Top reasons why people work with researchers

When we asked stakeholders what motivated them to work with researchers, these were the most common reasons people cited:
- Accessing future funding and new business opportunities
- Developing new solutions to old problems
- Increasing personal impact/influence through collaboration with researchers
- Intrinsic motivation to "make the world a better place" or a desire to learn about the issues being researched

Bear these motives in mind, and see if you can work out which of these motives apply to the people you want to work with. By tapping into their motives, and explaining clearly how working with you can achieve what they want, you are much more likely to get the level of engagement you want.

Resource your plan

Part of the impact planning process we will go through in Chapter 4 is about making sure you properly resource your plans for impact. Partly, this is simply about planning the knowledge exchange activities you want to do in detail, so that you can budget for them properly. But it is also about the staff resource you have to support impact. Although most research organisations now employ staff to support impact, it is rare that such staff can be deployed to specific projects, so you will need to make sure you have team members in place with the right skills. For larger projects, this may take the form of a paid position on the team.

For smaller projects (including PhD projects), this isn't possible, but you can still get help. It is often surprising how far a small budget can go if you can find a reasonable designer or consultant who has a track record of working with researchers (for example, take a look at Fast Track Impact's Design for Impact service). If you are really working on a small budget, then it is often surprising what skills there are around you, when you start looking. Reach out to others in your research group or graduate school. Offer what you're good at, and find out what others have got to offer. Perhaps you are a native English speaker and can help people proofread or write for generalist audiences, and there may be others in your group who are great at photography or have designed their own website.

Stay flexible

A good impact plan is not set in stone. Public interest in your field may suddenly peak as a result of a related issue in the news, and stakeholder needs and priorities change as they adapt to dynamic business and policy environments. So, it is useful if you can build an element of flexibility into the design of your research. This is really important because often, once your research design has been funded, you are expected to deliver it as it was designed. Building an element of flexibility into the design will help you justify changes you need to make as the research progresses, to accommodate the changing needs and priorities of those you are working with.

This is easier for some types of research than others. I was always told that reviewers would not look favourably on grant proposals that incorporated flexibility, but framed effectively I have found that a certain amount of flexibility actually attracts praise from reviewers.

You can still set ambitious goals and promise clear outcomes, but by incorporating flexibility, you can credibly claim to be able to adapt the research to the needs of those who will benefit, so they benefit more. For example, I often include an exploratory work package in which additional research questions and outcomes can be defined by stakeholders, and I will budget for events and dissemination materials that I do not yet know the focus of. If your plan for impact is flexible, you can be opportunistic, and exploit opportunities to communicate your research and generate impact as they arise. If you're locked into a plan that is too rigid to change, with no support or resources available when you need them, opportunities may pass you by.

Chapter 4
Principle 2: Represent

■■

Summary

Systematically represent the needs and priorities of those who will use your research:

- *Systematically identify individuals, groups, organisations and publics that are likely to be interested in, use or benefit from your research*
- *Identify stakeholders who could help or block you, or who might be disadvantaged by your work*
- *Revisit who you're working with as your context and stakeholder/public needs and interests change*
- *Embed key stakeholders in your research*
- *Consider the ethical implications of engaging with different stakeholders at different stages of the research cycle*

■■

As researchers, we are increasingly expected by funders to identify and incorporate 'beneficiaries' into our work from the outset. Working out who might benefit from our work isn't always easy though. Even if we know who will benefit from our research, an equally important but often unasked question is:

"Who might be disadvantaged or lose out as a result of my research?"

Even if we can answer both of these questions, there is another crucial question that every researcher should ask themselves:

"Who has the power to enable me to do my research and achieve impacts, and who has the power to block my work?"

37

It is just as important to identify individuals, organisations, groups and publics who might be disadvantaged by the outcomes of our work, or who may block our research, as it is to know who our beneficiaries are, and who can help us. I'm going to call these people 'stakeholders' and 'publics', rather than 'beneficiaries' (see Box 3 for my definition of stakeholders and publics). Knowing about potentially problematic stakeholders at the outset can give us the necessary time to adapt our research so that it no longer disadvantages those groups, or work out ways of mitigating negative impacts before we run into opposition or achieve bittersweet impacts for one group at the expense of another.

Analysing stakeholders

It may seem self-evident that all the relevant stakeholders should be identified prior to any attempt to engage. However, it is surprising how often this step is omitted in research projects that need to work with stakeholders. In many cases this omission can significantly compromise the success of the research. For example, the project may miss crucial information that could have been provided, had they engaged with the right people.

In cases where very few stakeholders are identified or engaged with, this can lead to a lack of ownership of project goals, which can sometimes turn into opposition from certain stakeholders. In cases where a single important stakeholder has been omitted from the process, that organisation or group may challenge the legitimacy of the work, and undermine the credibility of the wider project. Stakeholder analysis helps solve these problems by:

1. Identifying who has a stake in your work
2. Categorising and prioritising stakeholders you need to invest most time with
3. Identifying (and preparing you for) relationships between stakeholders (whether conflicts or alliances).

A successful stakeholder analysis will help you do six important things:

1. **Start talking early to the right people**, so that you can identify any major barriers to your work, and identify the people who can help you overcome those barriers. There is evidence that projects that engage with stakeholders early engender a greater sense of ownership amongst stakeholders, who are then more likely to engage throughout the lifetime of the project, and implement the recommendations of the work you have done together.
2. **Know who you need to talk to**: don't just open your address book or talk to the 'usual suspects'. Find out who might lose out, as well as who will benefit. Find out who is typically marginalised and left out, as well as the people and organisations that everyone knows and trusts. For example, you might draw on methods from the arts to identify stakeholders using tacit knowledge or past experience. Those who are left out are usually the first to question and criticise work that they feel no ownership over.
3. **Know what they're interested in**: you need to have a clear idea of the research issue at stake before you will be able to effectively identify stakeholders. But that doesn't mean that the research questions and issues you explore together should be set in stone. As you begin to identify stakeholders, you will find out more about the nature of their stake in your research, and you may need to broaden your view of what is included in your work, if everyone is to feel that their interests are included.
4. **Find out who's got the most influence** to help or hinder your work: some people, organisations or groups are more

powerful than others. If there are highly influential stakeholders who are opposed to your project, then you need to know who they are, so that you can develop an influencing strategy to win their support. If they support your work, then it is also important to know who these stakeholders are, so you can join forces with them to work more effectively. There will be some influential stakeholders who have relatively little interest in your work. For example, they may have a broad remit that includes many issues that are more important and urgent to them than the specific focus of your research. Influential individuals are often busy and inaccessible, and you may need to spend significant amounts of time and energy getting their attention, before you are able to access their help.

5. **Find out who is disempowered and marginalised**: stakeholder analysis is often used to prioritise more influential stakeholders for engagement. Although time and resources may be limited, it is important not to use stakeholder analysis as a tool to further marginalise groups that are already disempowered and ignored. Many of these groups may have a significant interest in your research, but very little influence over the issues you are researching, and little capacity to help you achieve the impacts you want.

6. **Identify key relationships so you avoid exacerbating conflicts and can create alliances** that empower marginalised groups. It can be incredibly valuable to know in advance about conflicts between individuals, organisations or groups, so that you can avoid inflaming conflict and where possible resolve disputes. Through stakeholder analysis, it can sometimes become possible to create alliances between disempowered groups and those with more power, who share similar interests and goals, thereby empowering previously marginalised groups.

For more detailed guidance on how to do stakeholder analysis, see Chapter 13.

Box 3: What are stakeholders and publics?

A stakeholder is any person, organisation or group that is affected by or can affect a decision, action or issue. Rather than just identifying 'beneficiaries', a stakeholder analysis seeks to identify people, organisations or groups who may be either positively or negatively affected by your research. In addition to identifying those affected by your research, stakeholder analysis seeks to also identify those who might affect your ability to complete your research and generate impacts, either positively or negatively. These stakeholders might not directly benefit from or be negatively affected by your work, but they may have the power to enable or block your work from making a difference. Stakeholder analysis is often used to identify and categorise different stakeholders for engagement, and is covered in more detail in Chapter 13.

Although everyone may be considered a member of the public in certain contexts, it is important to recognise that there are differences between individuals, by which we can group them e.g. backgrounds, affiliations, gender etc. Rather than thinking of the public as a single entity, it is useful to start thinking about different 'publics' if we want to identify groups who are more likely to be interested in our research. By targeting engagement activities towards these specific publics, it is possible to engage more efficiently and meaningfully. Audience segmentation is often used as a technique for identifying different publics, and is covered in more detail in Chapter 13.

Segmenting the public

If you want to efficiently and effectively engage with members of the public, it is important to understand who 'the public' is. Box 3 provides a definition, and emphasises the need to identify 'publics' that are more likely to be interested in your work, based on characteristics such as their background, interests, demographics, behaviours, media usage etc. Public segmentation techniques are based on audience segmentation techniques from marketing that group people based on characteristics that they share, which may be of relevance for marketing (e.g. targeting hair replacement treatments at men of a certain age). Chapter 13 explains this approach in more detail.

Chapter 5
Principle 3: Engage

■ ■

Summary

Build long-term, two-way, trusting relationships with those who will use your research and co-generate new knowledge together:
- *Have two-way dialogue as equals with likely users of your research*
- *Build long-term relationships with the users of your research*
- *Work with knowledge brokers and professional facilitators*
- *Understand what will motivate research users to get involved*
- *Work with stakeholders to interpret findings and co-design communication products*

■ ■

This principle sits in the middle of the other four principles, and it is central to any attempt to generate impact. In fact, if you wanted to boil my whole approach to impact down to a single word, it would be empathy. At the heart of this principle is the idea of really connecting with the people who might be interested in your research.

Empathy is understanding what it is like to think and feel like someone else. Or, as Barak Obama put it:

"I think we should talk more about our empathy deficit — the ability to put ourselves in someone else's shoes; to see the world through the eyes of those who are different from us — the child who's hungry, the steelworker who's been laid off, the family who lost the entire life they built together when the storm came to town. When you think like this, when you choose to broaden your ambit of concern and empathise with the plight of others, whether they are close friends or distant strangers; it becomes harder not to act; harder not to help."

43

If you can sense what it is like to be that other person, then you will know what motivates and inspires them, what worries and challenges them, and you will be able to find ways of making your research relevant to their needs and interests. No amount of tools and techniques can substitute for this skill. To paraphrase the apostle Paul, it doesn't matter how persuasively you craft your message, if you are unable to empathise with the people you're communicating with, then all they'll hear is noise.

Empathy is particularly important in situations where you need to deal with multiple competing agendas and personalities. The more ownership people feel over your research, the more likely it is that they may try and exert influence over the research process and outcomes. Where these suggestions might compromise the rigour of our research, it is clear that we should not follow them. However, many suggestions could take us down equally legitimate and interesting routes, and by following these paths, we may be able to effect significant change that benefits many. The problem is that different stakeholders may have competing visions of the path they

would like the project to take, for example, focusing on different case studies or focal issues. Add to this long-standing conflicts between different individuals and organisations, and you've got a challenging meeting on your hands. Negotiating between these competing agendas will be tricky, and will require every bit of emotional intelligence you can summon up.

Sometimes that connection happens over the research, and sometimes it might be over a picture on their wall or a book on their shelf. The point is, that I'm trying to understand something about what really makes them tick; what gets them up in the morning and keeps them going. If it's not obvious, then I will ask people indirectly at first, with questions like, "What took you into this role? What is it that you love most about what you do? What is it about this organisation or task (or whatever it is that they are doing) that you love?". Then more directly, I may ask what sort of unanswered questions (relating to my field of enquiry) they have, what are their goals, and what knowledge or help do they need to reach those goals, individually or as an organisation. Usually there is something somewhere in the answers to those questions that enables me to connect them to my research or a colleague, and something that enables me to connect with them at some slightly deeper level too.

The second thing that I think we can do to cultivate empathy is to be humble in our interactions with stakeholders and the public. It is remarkably easy to fall into the trap of living up to people's expectations, without even realising that you're doing it. If someone expects you to act like the know-it-all expert who will give them all the answers, social conditioning creates a strong subconscious desire to meet that expectation (especially when doing so is likely to give you an ego-boost at the same time). Resist that temptation. A simple expression of humility, for example, telling someone that you don't know the answer to their question, and that you would genuinely like to hear their opinion, can instantly break down barriers, and build trust and rapport. When it becomes clear from your questions and your behaviour that you genuinely want your research to help them, and it's not just about building your career and ego, people start to tentatively offer small things that you might be able to help with. No matter how small that first request is, if you can do everything in your power to help, and go the extra mile, you will gain enough trust to be asked to help with something bigger.

Many research programmes now offer formal opportunities for researchers and stakeholders to work more closely together, for example, via work shadowing, placements and fellowships. These are invaluable opportunities for understanding stakeholder organisations and their cultures, and for demonstrating the benefits that your research can bring them. If there aren't any formal opportunities you can apply for, then create your own opportunities to connect with people through the events you attend, and the way you design events (e.g. providing sufficiently long breaks, designing activities to get different people working in small groups together, or opportunities to talk *en route* to a site visit).

It is these long-term, trusting and two-way relationships that foster knowledge exchange and ultimately lead to impact. People talk of creating 'safe spaces' for collaboration with stakeholders, but no matter how well you design your workshop, you can offer little safety as a stranger. It is those trusting relationships that actually persuade people to come to the workshop in the first place, and it is those trusting relationships that become the life-blood of your impact between events and other interactions.

If you can afford it, professional facilitation is one of the most important factors leading to successful outcomes from workshops with stakeholders (Box 4). A professional facilitator can help create spaces for constructive dialogue and collaboration between research teams and stakeholders, especially in situations where there is conflict or controversy.

If you can't afford professional facilitation, there are still a lot of simple things you can do to design meetings and events that effectively facilitate themselves. Part 4 provides a range of tools and techniques that you can use to design events with stakeholders so that you can easily keep a handle on the power dynamics and prevent things getting out of control. Broadly speaking, I progress through the following types of techniques when I'm designing a workshop (for detailed examples of methods in each category, see Chapter 14):

- **Opening out**: There are a number of techniques for opening up dialogue and gathering information with stakeholders about issues linked to your research. This collection of techniques is particularly useful during the initial phases of a research project, either during the development of initial research questions prior to writing a funding proposal, or in the early phases of a funded project, where the research goals and programme of work are being adapted to better fit the needs and interests of stakeholders.
- **Exploring**: There are a range of methods that can help you evaluate and analyse preliminary findings with stakeholders. Given the length of most research projects, getting early feedback on preliminary findings can help keep stakeholders interested in the process and give them greater ownership over the eventual research outcomes. The feedback can also provide researchers with ideas about how to further refine their work, such as where assumptions are not clear or are questioned by stakeholders.
- **Deciding**: After issues have been opened out and analysed, it is often necessary to start closing down options and deciding on actions based on research findings. There are a number of techniques that can engage researchers and stakeholders in decisions based on research findings, for example, prioritising particularly interesting or relevant findings for further research or action.

I also believe that a few tips as a facilitator can go a long way if you don't have a lot of experience. Although there is no substitute for experience in this game, having a Plan B (and C) and a few ways of dealing with challenging individuals can turn a scary situation into a productive and enjoyable event for everyone. Chapter 15 provides lots of practical advice on facilitating workshops with stakeholders.

Similarly, knowledge brokers and intermediaries can help facilitate dialogue. Knowledge brokers work like bridges between disparate social networks and can significantly speed up the process of gaining trust. Effective knowledge brokers are typically well known and trusted by many different groups, and have an interest in your research. It may be worth creating official roles for such individuals in the research, such as including them in advisory panels or being involved in hosting or co-designing events. Because they are known and trusted by many of the stakeholders you want to work with, if you are introduced or recommended by this intermediary, people are much more likely to trust you.

Box 4: Three secrets of successful stakeholder engagement

As part of the British Academy-funded Involved project, I recently investigated 24 projects in 20 different countries in which researchers worked with stakeholders, in an attempt to work out the most important factors that enabled those processes to achieve their goals. Three things emerged from the analysis that were more important than anything else:

- Represent all the relevant stakeholders;
- Get a professional facilitator to help you manage power dynamics between stakeholders; and
- Empower stakeholders with information and decision-making power, so they can meaningfully participate in your research.

The groups that got these three things right were not only more likely to achieve the goals they had established together, but they were also more likely to report having learned and gained trust in the other participants as a result of their experience. The networks and alliances that can arise from such interaction may yield impacts many years after your initial work together.

Finally, working with stakeholders to identify and articulate the implications of research for policy and practice can help researchers target their communication effectively and enhance the probability that the target audience interprets findings appropriately. Co-designing communication materials with stakeholders can increase the likelihood that other stakeholders engage with the material, and the process of co-developing materials may facilitate learning, both among stakeholders (about the research) and researchers (about how to communicate more effectively with particular groups). If it is possible to get research users and stakeholders to disseminate these communication materials themselves, this may further increase their reach.

Chapter 6
Principle 4: Early Impacts

▪▪▪

Summary

Deliver tangible results as soon as possible to keep people engaged with your work. Identify quick wins where tangible impacts can be delivered as early as possible in the research process, to reward and keep likely users of research engaged with the research process.

▪▪▪

One of the key challenges of achieving impact from research is the timescale over which most research projects operate. At best, most research projects take 3 years to complete, but some last longer, and it is often closer to 5 years before findings are actually published in the peer-reviewed literature. In contrast to this, most businesses, practitioners and policy-makers need knowledge to address specific needs over timescales measured in days, weeks or months. If you are working with members of the public, providing benefits early in your research can enable them to shape your research and stay involved throughout the course of your research project, rather than just at the end. Early engagement can peak people's interest in your research and build contacts and mailing lists you can use later on to engage these same groups with your research findings.

The first challenge then is to manage expectations about the timescales over which you will be able to deliver findings, making it clear that you will not be able to deliver *final* results till the end of the project, which is typically years later. Once you have overcome this hurdle, the next challenge is to retain people's interest and engagement, as you get on with the hard work of doing your research. I've been involved in projects where we engaged with people at the start to set the agenda and then didn't get back in touch again till we'd finished the research. For us, every day brought a new challenge, and we were so busy that it felt like very little time had passed before we contacted people again. By contrast, people reacted with surprise that we were still there, still doing the research — many had assumed that we'd forgotten all about them and their concerns. In the intervening period, many of them had moved on — to other jobs and other

51

concerns. Had we stayed in touch, the people who had moved into their roles would have known about our research, and we'd have had a chance to adapt our research to their changing needs and preferences.

So, how can you deliver tangible outcomes for people early in a project, before you've actually done the research? I'm not suggesting that you compromise the rigour of your research by leaking early findings to the press before you've gone through the proper ethical and peer-review processes. I think that there are a number of creative ways you can answer this question without compromising your ethics or the quality of your work, that can help keep people motivated and engaged in your research (Box 5).

I think the first answer to this question is to recognise that people value research for its ability to provide them with answers to questions; knowledge that is new *to them*, relevant, interesting and useful. As researchers, we are so focused on the generation of completely new knowledge that we forget that our knowledge of the discipline already enables us to answer many of the questions that people care most about. I think we often forget the privileged position we sit in, behind journal pay walls, with an understanding of the jargon that enables us to access the latest knowledge in our field as it is published. Many of the people who most need this knowledge are unable to justify paying to access the research, and even when they do, they find the language impenetrable.

Just by making our own existing knowledge accessible (let alone the latest knowledge in our field), we can immediately add value. For example:

- **Run workshops, exhibitions, performances or other events about the general subject area of your research** (for example an author or composer's work, or hearing perceptions), to build connections and mailing lists of relevant groups who are likely to be interested in your work, once research findings become available (for example about a particular aspect of that author's work, or your new audiology research)
- **Crowd-fund a product or performance related to your research in your first year.** The crowd-funding will give you the resources to run this as a mini-project in parallel with your main research, and you then have a diverse and interested audience who you can contact with future updates

and events related to your research (see chapter 18 for more information about crowdfunding research)

- **Make your review of the 'state of the art' from your funding proposal available as a briefing note with links to the latest literature.** Most of us have already reviewed the latest literature as part of our research proposal before we even started doing the work. Can you make this short review of the 'state of the art' in your field available in accessible language to people who are interested in your work? You can even do this from failed research proposals — the research you proposed may not have been good enough to get funded, but there was probably nothing wrong with your review of the literature in the field (depending on how original your perspective is on the literature, you can even turn this into a 'response' to one of the key articles you've reviewed, and contribute to the peer-reviewed literature — I've done this)

- **Turn the literature review you did at the start of the project into a briefing note.** Most research projects start by reviewing the literature in greater depth, but these reviews end up buried in PhD theses or are condensed to form a section of a paper that only appears years later in an inaccessible journal. Can you turn your literature review into a briefing note for stakeholders or send it to a freelance journalist to see if they can help you turn it into a feature piece for a weekend newspaper or magazine? I once got into some trouble with a piece of government-funded research I was advising on, where the commissioning officer was upset at the lack of progress in the project. As far as the team were concerned, they were just getting on with the research, but there was nothing to show for their work yet. I had reviewed the literature in order to be able to advise the team, but the review I'd sent them was highly technical. So I suggested that I turn my review into a couple of policy briefs. I didn't have time to do any design or polishing, but that evening I created two briefs and by the next day the policy team were loving the project and already moving forward in their thinking about the issue. If you're not sure how to write a policy brief, go to Chapter 20
- **Write a newsletter**, and don't worry if there's no news to report from your project. Doing a monthly or quarterly survey of the latest news and peer-reviewed literature relating to your project is a good habit to get into anyway. The chances are that you're getting all this information delivered to your email inbox and social media accounts anyway, and incorporating that knowledge into your mental model of the issues you're researching. Creating lay summaries of key papers is a great way of honing your generalist communication skills, and it often surprises me how much this helps me understand and remember a paper I've read. Once you've done this, you can instantly share the key insights in a form that's easy to understand with a link to the original paper on social media. You can also harvest news stories from social media that others may not have come across and link to these from your newsletter. I've published project newsletters during quiet periods where we're just getting on with the research, which have very little project-specific news, but that retain interest and create value for stakeholders by reporting the latest news in our field. Although this takes time, in addition to adding value for your

stakeholders, you'll be surprised how much value it adds to your research, if you have to always be on the cutting edge of what's happening in your field

Box 5: Seven easy ways to achieve early impacts

Try the following ideas in your research to achieve early impacts and keep stakeholders engaged with your work for the long term:
1. Make your review of the 'state of the art' from your funding proposal available as a briefing note with links to the latest literature in accessible language
2. Turn the literature review you did at the start of the project into a briefing note (or two)
3. Write a newsletter, supplementing your work with other updates in your field based on your reading and engagement with sources via social media
4. Create a powerful and useful social media presence for your research that really helps people
5. Reframe your research as press releases to link to the latest headlines and topical issues
6. Coordinate research milestones with the milestones stakeholders are working towards
7. Make data and models available where feasible

- **Create a powerful and useful social media presence for your research.** Consider how useful your social media presence is for those interested in your research. If you already have a well-focused group of people enjoying what you do, and you want to reach out more widely, consider creating new social media accounts that specifically target particular groups or reach out to the public, and promote these from your main accounts. I once created a Twitter account for a research project that became one of the most influential in its field, and was eventually rebranded and taken over by an international NGO after the project ended. Of course, I've also created accounts that were never really noticed by anyone. But with a clear social media strategy, it is surprising how much value you can add by promoting research and evidence in an easily accessible way. You can find out about how to create a social media strategy for your research in Chapter 16

- **Reframe your research as press releases to link to the latest headlines and topical issues.** If you are aware of the latest issues hitting the news, you will be well placed to adapt or reframe your research, so that you can put out a press release that links to a particularly topical issue, that is far more likely to get your work media coverage. It was this sort of media coverage (linking peat bogs to issues of climate change) that initiated the impact I described at the start of Chapter 2

- **Coordinate milestones** in your research with the milestones that your stakeholders are working towards. If you know about a forthcoming policy review, election or issue-based campaign, product launch or event in the diary of those you're working with, it is sometimes possible to reorganise your research to provide relevant findings in time. Moving your data collection forward by a month may be relatively easy for your team, and could make the difference between being able to contribute to the development of a new policy or product, or not. If you don't know about these milestones till they are almost on top of you, there is often very little you can do to provide meaningful contributions in time

- Depending on your field, and the ethics procedures you need to go through, it can sometimes be possible to **make data and models available to stakeholders** to analyse and test themselves. For example, you may not have time to produce anything meaningful before a deadline in the policy world, but policy analysts may be very grateful to have access to data that they can run their own analysis on to brief their minister before a debate.

It is important to regularly discuss your work with stakeholders if you want to make sure you are producing work that will still deliver relevant impacts, and to spot opportunities to add value as you conduct your work. These people will quickly tell you if their agendas have moved on and they are now looking for different things from your work — if you ask them. They will also be able to tell you how to make your work as accessible as possible, so as many people as possible can benefit from it. For example, in one project I was managing, we were planning to use Geographical Information Systems to show people how a landscape was likely to change in the future. We thought that this would be really accessible because it visualised some fairly complex model outputs in pretty colours on a map. However, when we took this idea to our stakeholder advisory panel, they told us that they found this really abstract and difficult to get their heads around. Instead they asked us why we couldn't just make a documentary film to explain it. This took some additional funding, which we were able to find by juggling our project budget a bit, but it was actually a very easy request to meet. Those films have now been watched thousands of times on You Tube, giving us far more reach than we could have had using maps in workshops. This illustrates the first principle (design, Chapter 3), where I spoke about the importance of building flexibility into your project and having stakeholders embedded in your work.

Finally, it is important to stress under this principle that I'm not advocating unofficial publication of results prior to proper quality control. Many researchers have been tempted to release findings early when their topic has hit the headlines, and regret their actions when they later discover flaws in their work, which would have been ironed out if they had waited. Sometimes you have to let opportunities go, and trust that other opportunities will arise once you are confident that your findings are ready to be made public. In cases where you think it is acceptable to provide preliminary findings or data to stakeholders for their own internal uses, it is important to consider carefully how you communicate risk and uncertainty relating to your work, to avoid misleading people. In some cases, if you are taking a co-productive approach to your work, key stakeholders will be embedded within your team, with access to data. What happens to your data then comes down to trust, which emphasises the importance of the previous principle (engage, Chapter 5).

One project I was leading was co-funded by both the government and an NGO that was opposing the government on the issue we were researching. I received some very worried emails from civil servants when it became clear that our findings contradicted government policy ahead of a major policy announcement. At the same time, I received emails from the NGO saying that they thought they could get front-page news headlines based on our research, which would help them achieve their goals. There was sufficient trust in the team however, that I was able to speak to the head of the NGO and suggest that they would be more likely to change government policy if they worked constructively with the civil servants who had jointly commissioned the work because they wanted to base their work on the best possible evidence. The policy announcement went ahead (but with the caveat that it would be revisited and possibly changed in future) and was denounced by the NGO without reference to our research. Then, over the following year, the NGO and others worked with government using our evidence and other research, and the policy ended up being changed.

So, have a think about how you can provide early impacts from your research — but not too early. You may be surprised how much value you can add already.

Chapter 7
Principle 5: Reflect and Sustain

. . . .

Summary

Keep track of your progress towards impact, so you can improve your knowledge exchange, and continue nurturing relationships and generating impacts in the long term:
- *Track your impacts*
- *Regularly reflect on your knowledge exchange with research team and stakeholders*
- *Learn from peers and share good practice*
- *Identify what knowledge exchange needs to continue after the end of the project and consider how to generate long-term impacts*

. . . .

How do you know your research is having an impact, and who knows about your impact? Although these questions seem simple to answer, researchers and institutions around the world are scratching their heads, trying to work out how to actually monitor the impacts they are having on the world around them.

The last principle is all about becoming a reflective practitioner of knowledge exchange and impact. I can't think of a single example of research impact that did not involve some sort of knowledge exchange. Therefore, as I said in Chapter 2, if you want to have an impact, you need to be great at knowledge exchange. If you want to be great at knowledge exchange, then you need to take time to reflect on your activities and get feedback. Tracking impact is also often required by funders and governments who want to see the impact that their money is having. The same information can also be used for marketing purposes, and to target resources and support to the researchers and teams who need it most. By sharing good practice across an institution, it becomes possible to celebrate individual and collective success and learn, so that everyone can work together to make a bigger difference.

You may be motivated to track the impact of your research for a number of quite different reasons. As individual researchers, many of us are motivated extrinsically to demonstrate impact so that we can get on in our career. We may be intrinsically motivated to see if we are achieving our personal goals, so we can learn how to make more of a difference. Research and impact managers in our institutions may want us to track impact so they can understand how to target help to those of us who have the potential to make a difference. Much of this is extrinsically motivated by the need to achieve high scores in impact evaluations that will feed into rankings, reputation and financial rewards for the institution. Although much of this might feel like game-playing, and probably is, I have yet to meet a knowledge exchange professional in an impact-orientated role who gets their kicks from playing the game. Ultimately, our goal collectively is to help each other raise our game to make our research more relevant and change more lives for the better. If we can change the narrative from bean-counting to progress-watching, then more of us might be persuaded that impact can go far beyond promotions and rankings. Tracking impact might become more about sharing good practice and inspiring each other to go the extra mile. After all, the impacts we leave from our research are a huge part of our legacy. As Jackie Robinson, the first African American to play Major League Baseball, put it:

"A life is not important except in the impact it has on other people's lives."

The challenges of tracking impact are not trivial. There are particular problems with attributing impacts to specific research findings, which are exacerbated by time lags between the production of knowledge through research and its application and impact. There are also challenges associated with how impact is defined and perceived, both by researchers and those we work with. There are concerns that current attempts by research funders and governments to measure and reward impact may be funnelling effort into a narrow range of socially constructed impacts that are considered by researchers to really matter.

I was recently part of a team that reviewed 135 evaluations of knowledge exchange and impact across diverse disciplines. We found that researchers in different disciplines defined impact quite differently, and hence looked for quite different things in their attempts to track it. Partly this is simply due to the fact that some disciplines (e.g. many from the arts and humanities) focus more on public engagement and education, while others focus on more instrumental impacts. However, we found that one of the most important things determining people's definition of impact and how they measured it was their perception of what constitutes valid knowledge (what social scientists refer to as 'epistemology'). Those with a more 'positivist' perspective tended to focus on more one-way, knowledge transfer to achieve impacts, and were more likely to track impact using quantitative methods. Those with more 'subjectivist' perspectives, in contrast, were more likely to run knowledge exchange activities that encouraged mutual learning through multi-stakeholder interactions. People who viewed knowledge in this way were more likely to track impact using methods that captured the diverse experiences of those involved and were more likely to consider a wider range of factors that may have contributed to impacts.

I think this calls for some fairly deep reflection, which may not be comfortable for all of us. How do you think knowledge is generated and what do you consider to be valid knowledge, from which impacts should arise? What then do you think are the most relevant ways of tracking your impact?

Whether you come from a more subjectivist or positivist school of thought, there are two broad types of approach to tracking impact: summative and normative (Box 6). Try and get a balance between both, but make sure that you've got good formative feedback available to help you improve your practice.

Box 6: Two approaches to tracking impact

There are two broad types of approach to tracking impact:
- **Summative** tracking and evaluation of impacts after they have occurred with minimal participation of researchers or beneficiaries, to provide ex-post measures of reach and significance
- **Formative** tracking and evaluation of knowledge exchange and impact in collaboration with researchers and beneficiaries, to provide ongoing feedback on reach and significance, so that impacts can be enhanced during the research cycle

The majority of impact tracking and evaluation is done in the first, summative, ex-post mode by research funders to evaluate the impact of their investments or to distribute quality-rated funding to the best research institutions. However, it is also worth investing in formative tracking of impacts as they arise, including an on-going evaluation of the knowledge exchange activities that are meant to deliver those impacts.

Getting formative feedback on your knowledge exchange and impact

Broadly speaking there are two main sources of formative feedback if you want to reflect upon and improve your knowledge exchange practice. First, feedback from colleagues can be incredibly helpful — these are the people who you can (hopefully) trust to be constructively honest with you when things really didn't work, and who can support you to improve your practice. I like to schedule time for a debrief with my research team after any kind of knowledge exchange activity, even if this is an online activity, so we can discuss what went well and what could have been done better.

Second, some of the most valuable feedback can come from the members of the public and stakeholders we were trying to engage with. Often, a survey at or after an event can give you the feedback you need, but sometimes you just need to pick up the phone or meet up for a drink with someone to find out in depth what went wrong or right. If you wait till the end of your project to ask people, it may be too late to correct simple issues (like the time of day you were engaging with people) that could have made a massive difference to the levels of engagement with your research.

As discussed in the previous principle (early impacts, Chapter 6), checking in regularly with stakeholders can also help you identify new opportunities for generating impact that you would not have spotted if you hadn't sought their feedback. Also, by building in opportunities for regular feedback about your knowledge exchange activities throughout the project, it may be possible to reassess who holds a stake or is likely to use the research, to ensure that stakeholder representation remains relevant throughout the research cycle (represent, Chapter 4).

Where possible, involve stakeholders who have engaged with the research in the evaluation of your knowledge exchange activities. The evaluation process provides opportunities for stakeholders to work together to share perspectives, increase ownership of and responsibility for knowledge exchange, and enables participants to work together to refine your practice. The challenge is to develop evaluation processes that facilitate achievement of desired goals, provide valid and reliable data for ongoing planning and decision-making processes, and contribute to open and accountable research governance.

Track and build your impact for the long term

If you've developed an impact plan for your research (see the first principle, engage, in Chapter 3 and the template in Part 4 of this book), then you should have some simple metrics you can monitor to keep track of your impact. I will discuss how you can evidence your impact in more detail in Chapter 21. However, given the time lags and other factors that can affect your impact, it is just as important to track the success of your knowledge exchange (see the indicator column in the impact planning tool in Part 4). If you monitor your knowledge exchange, you can improve your practice, and enhance the likelihood that your research actually does lead to impacts.

Substantial benefits can be derived for many stakeholders after projects have been completed, through ongoing communication and interpretation of findings. Where possible, 'legacy arrangements' can support continued engagement between researchers and research users, to extract and augment value from the previous research through interpretation activities and supplementary analysis. It can help if the timescale over which engagement needs to be sustained is considered from the outset. For example, if a project plans to develop a network that will have the potential to work together beyond the time frame of the initial project, it will be necessary to forge collaborations with organisations who share this goal, but who can also fund or administer such a network long after the project has ended.

Despite wanting to move my research from Africa to the UK after my PhD to avoid becoming an absentee father, I maintained relationships with those I worked with, and got funding to follow up my research through the production of manuals in local languages for agricultural advisors and farmers. This has led to a steady flow of opportunities to work with the policy community, which in turn have spawned a steady flow of academic publications. Partly because of the expertise that these publications demonstrated, but I suspect partly also because of my reputation for public speaking, this led to invitations to speak at two major United Nations policy conferences. What has surprised me is how little effort it took to keep these relationships alive, and add value despite this no longer being a major focus of my research. People are thirsty for knowledge, and hungry for people who can give it to them in palatable forms.

Part 2: Steps to fast track your impact

Chapter 8
Step 1: Envision your impact

∎∎∎

Summary

This first step will help you fast track your impact by understanding the sorts of impacts that your research might be able to generate. You will need to come up with a core goal and understand the motives behind why you want your research to have more of an impact. Finally, you will break this ultimate goal down into a series of smaller steps that you can take over the coming weeks and months in your research.

∎∎∎

Five steps to fast track your impact

Understanding each of the five principles in the preceding chapters is essential if you want to take a relational approach to impact that has far-reaching and long-lasting effects. Although some of the principles are a little abstract, I've tried to illustrate each of them with practical things I've done, and which you can also do to enact each principle in your own research. But actually taking these principles and putting them into action can be hard for some people without a bit more structure. So I've developed five steps based on these principles that can enable you to change the way you do research, so you achieve impact.

This will work best if you have a research project in mind that you'd like to derive impacts from. I recommend that you take about a week to think through each step and try out the tasks in your own research. This gives you the opportunity to learn about impact in the specific context of your own research discipline, and gain confidence as you try things out in the real world, one step at a time. These steps are based on evidence I've collected over my decade of research on impact. They are also based on my own personal experience, and the experience of the many researchers I've worked with to take their impact to new levels. They really do work — try them out.

If you want extra help with these steps, you can sign up to receive each step via email every week over five weeks on the Fast Track Impact website (www.fasttrackimpact.com). I'll talk you through each step in a short video, and I'll give you personal help with your ideas for impact.

These are the steps (Figure 5):
1. **Envision** your impact
2. **Plan** for impact
3. **Cut back** anything hindering or distracting you from your impact
4. **Get specific** about the impacts you will seek and the people who can help you achieve impact this month
5. **Achieve** your first step towards impact and monitor your success

This chapter introduces the first step, and the subsequent four short chapters explain each of the other steps. First, let me outline the steps and explain how they build on each of the principles we've looked at so far.

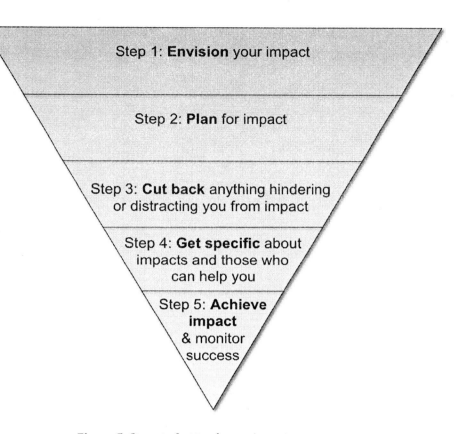

Figure 5: Steps to fast track your impact.

Step 1: Envision your impact

Understanding the impacts of our research is obvious for some, but it is incredibly tricky for many of us. By the end of this step, you will have a clear idea of the types of impacts that your research might be able to generate.

I'll start by walking you through a series of questions designed to draw out the potential impacts of your work. Then we'll begin to focus on your core goal and start to interrogate some of the motives behind this goal. And finally, we will break this ultimate goal of your research into less intimidating, more immediate staging posts that can keep you motivated and on track.

Eight questions to identify your impacts

So, what impact do you think your research might be able to generate? If you are working on applied, real-world issues in your research, this question might be obvious. Sadly, for most of us, it is far from being the case. So I've developed these questions to try and walk you through a process that should start to identify the potential impacts that could arise from your research:

1. What aspects of your research might be interesting or useful to someone, or could you (or someone else) build upon to create something interesting or useful at some point in the future?
2. Going beyond your research for a moment, think of issues, policy areas, sectors of the economy, practices, behaviours, trends etc. that link in some way to your research. What problems or needs are there in these places, and what are the barriers that are preventing these issues from being resolved? Could your research help address these needs and barriers in some way?
3. What is the most significant area of current policy, practice or business that your research might change or disrupt?
4. Which are the individuals, groups or organisations that might be interested in this aspect of your research (whether now or in future)?
5. What aspects of your research are they likely to be most interested in, and what would need to happen for this to become more relevant to them? What could you do differently to make your work more relevant to these people? Who would you need help from?

6. If these people took an interest in or used your research, what would change?
7. Might you see changes in individuals, groups, organisations, or at a societal or some other level?
8. Would these changes be beneficial or might some groups be disadvantaged in some way as a result of your research?

We'll think more about how you can avoid negative impacts in the next step. So for now, please list as many benefits as possible for each of the different groups you identified in question 4. Now go through this list of benefits, grouping similar benefits together and turning them into impact objectives. Make your objectives SMART: specific, measurable, achievable, realistic and time-bound. For example, contrast these two impact objectives:

- To curate a highly successful exhibition of work discovered as a result of my research (not very SMART)
- To curate and successfully market an exhibition of work discovered as a result of my research that will attract in excess of 10,000 visitors to the gallery by the end of the exhibition, and that will reach audiences across the UK and in at least 3 other countries via coverage in mass media and articles in specialist magazines (measured in column inches) and internationally via social media and online content production (measured via engagement metrics) (SMART)

Getting clear on your goal

At this point, you should have a number of different impact goals. Now, if you could only achieve one of these goals, which would it be? Which one is most important to you?

There are no rights or wrongs here. A goal may be important for you for purely personal reasons. For example, you might prioritise an impact goal that is likely to help you score highly when your research gets assessed, and will help you get a promotion. Or you might want to choose the goal that you believe will make the biggest difference to the issues and people you care most about.

The first thing that we are trying to do here, is to get really specific and focused about what it is that we want to achieve. It is often surprising how opportunities suddenly appear that help you achieve a goal when you bring that goal very clearly into focus. This is probably nothing more than the fact that we notice things that can help us achieve that goal, which we would have otherwise missed. When you have a clear vision of where you are going, it is possible to cut out much of the noise that has been holding us back and creating confusion. We start to see clearly what it is that we need to do.

What is motivating you to have an impact?

The second thing I want you to do, is to work out what is really important to you personally about generating impact. The chances are that if you really analyse why it is that you have chosen this particular impact goal, you will find that it links in some way to your personal priorities, values or beliefs. Perhaps you need to get that promotion so you can move to a larger house because you want to have children, and it is those family values that are driving your desire to engage with the impact agenda. Perhaps it is simply ego; you want a legacy you can be proud of. If these are the sorts of values that are motivating your engagement with impact, then you need to pay very careful attention to the identification of risks in the next step. The reality is that all of us have complex and mixed motives for most of the things we do, but if personal benefit is a big motivator, there is a danger that you may end up inadvertently creating negative unintended consequences in your attempts to generate impact. You would probably never think this consciously (although I was once in a stakeholder workshop with a senior academic who actually said this out loud), but you may be 'using' stakeholders to achieve your own goals, and as a result, stakeholders may well feel used.

Of course, our motives are usually mixed in everything we do, and ego and other personal benefits are usually part of that mix. We need to get a healthy balance of motivations driving our desire to make a difference, and make sure that we are not only or primarily being driven by our egos. Being clear about our motives can really strengthen our motivation to generate impact. Bringing the complexity of our motives to consciousness can also help us to avoid some of the abuses of impact that many commentators have warned might happen if academics become more extrinsically incentivised to generate impact. And by focusing clearly on the myriad reasons why we are doing what we are doing, we are more likely to be able to pick ourselves up again when things go wrong, as they inevitably will at some point.

Where can you create most value?

I personally believe that rather than focusing on what we can get personally from engaging with impact, it is much more empowering to ask what we can give that produces value. Rather than remaining in a place of insufficiency, by focusing on what we do not have, this second question comes from a place of abundance and strength, which builds your confidence and empowers you to make a difference. I believe that most of the people who have achieved most in academia have been those who have given the most.

Their secret is strategic giving; they give to others who, like them, also give, rather than to those who consistently only take. That's not to say we should not mentor and help those who cannot give anything to us in return, that we should marginalise those less fortunate than ourselves, or that we should be calculating the time in terms of a return on investment. It does, however, mean that you might want to take a strategic look at whether some of the relationships you are investing most time in for your work are actually taking you away from spending time achieving your core goals. There may be very little you can do at this point but, if nothing else, it may be a lesson for the future (e.g. not to take on weak PhD students who aren't working in areas that are central to your research interests).

If you want to be successful at achieving impact, then give to others. Seek out how you can add value and help, and do all this in an attitude of humility, being open to learn from those you work with.

What will you achieve in the next six months?

The problem with the sorts of goals that many of us are trying to reach to make an impact is that they are often a long way off; in some cases, a very, very long way off. We probably all have experience with very long-term goals; they have a habit of not happening. Things change; we change. Other things become more important.

So in addition to whatever your ultimate impact goal might be, no matter how far off or challenging it may be to achieve, I want to bring your focus closer to home now. I would like you to try and come up with some specific goals that are no more than six months in the future, but which are still closely linked to your ultimate goal. These will be staging posts on the journey to your goal, and they will keep you motivated and provide you with feedback, to keep you on track. The more detail with which you can visualise these goals, the more useful these short-term goals are likely to be. If you can, imagine yourself having just reached that staging post and see what it looks and feels like in your mind's eye.

Coming up with short-term impact goals

There are a number of ways you can come up with these short-term goals, but I'm going to suggest two that have worked for me. First, you can 'backcast' from your goal. As the name suggests, this is the opposite of forecasting. Start with the ultimate impact you want to achieve from your research, and then use your imagination to think of the step that would come immediately before having reached that goal. In the same way, keep stepping back, till you get to smaller initial steps that you might be able to take in the next six months.

The second approach works the opposite way around. Instead of working back from the end point, you need to look at where you are now in relation to your goal. The first thing you are doing is to identify everything you can that you've already done that has put you in a position to be able to pursue this impact goal, for example, you've got a funded research project and a team with some useful skills.

Maybe you already have some really relevant relationships and have a clear understanding of what research needs to be done before you could have an impact. These are all strong foundations upon which you can build, and rather than looking at all your weaknesses, problems and barriers to achieving impact, you are moving into a more empowering place that recognises the strengths and achievements you can build on.

Build on your strengths and successes

From this position of strength then, you can then begin to see all the skills, insights and resources at your disposal, with which you might be able to add value to someone else who is on a similar journey. It can be useful to actually create a list of your skills and strengths. In Box 7, you can find questions to help you identify and build on your strengths for impact.

Apart from being a useful exercise for building your CV, this can be an enriching and revealing process; especially if you do it with someone who knows you well. In addition to the things that come immediately to mind, for example, areas of expertise in which you are highly knowledgeable or methods and equipment you can use, this exercise will enable you to identify other things that might not be so obvious. For example, do you enjoy photography or art in your spare time? Might you be able to take some of that creative flair into your impact work to add value to someone else? When you start to really look for places where these skills can add value, it is often surprising how many opportunities will present themselves to you. For example, there may be an NGO or business working in a similar area with similar goals, which could really benefit from your expertise. By adding value to others and giving in this targeted way, you open the door to powerful new relationships and collaborative possibilities that would otherwise not have been available.

Box 7: Building on your strengths

Answer these questions yourself or with someone you know well.
It can work particularly well if you do this in a pair with someone you
know well, and then swap answers, and discuss. You will often find
that your partner is able to identify many additional strengths you
may not have been aware of.

1. Describe one of your greatest successes
Describe a high-point experience during the last year when you felt
most alive, engaged, or really proud of yourself and your work.

2. What are your strengths and skills?
Thinking of this experience, or another recent achievement in your
work, identify what strengths and skills you brought to this
experience that enabled it to be such a success. Consider strengths
and skills you use in your work, and outside your work, and whether
or not you can see an obvious way yet that these skills could help
you generate impact.

3. What do you value most?
What do you most value about yourself and your job? Rather than
just adding to your list of strengths and skills, consider whether
there are some more fundamental things about who you are as a
person and the role you play in your work that drive your success.
These could be aspects of your personality or deeply held values
and beliefs about yourself or the world.

**4. What strengths can you build on to achieve even greater
success?**
Drawing on all the strengths, skills, expertise and value you know
you bring to your work, identify strengths you believe you can either:
i) enhance and make even stronger; or ii) complement with new
skills and strengths in future. Then consider the actions you could
take to enhance or build upon your strengths.

If you are really struggling to come up with any sort of specific impact goal for your research, simply looking for ways to add value with what you have got, can often be the first step towards finding a tangible impact. By forming relationships with others outside the academy who are working in related areas, we often make mental connections between our research and the context these organisations are working in, which would not have been possible if we had not reached out.

Your tasks for the first step

1   Work through the eight questions at the beginning of this chapter to identify your impact.
2   Choose your most important impact and be able to explain why it is important to you.
3   Identify at least one thing you could do in the next six months that would help you reach your most important impact goal.

Chapter 9
Step 2: Plan for impact

■■■

Summary

In this step, you will become clear about who might benefit from your research and how you can engage with them to achieve impact, using an impact plan. Creating an impact plan using the template in Part 4 of this book is incredibly easy. It may take anywhere between an hour and half a day to come up with a first draft, but investing time in this step will save days and days of time later, by ensuring you don't waste time on activities that don't actually help you achieve your impacts. By taking this step, you will turn impact from a possibility into an inevitability. Follow your plan, and you will achieve impacts.

■■■

Most research funders now require researchers to develop an effective 'Pathway to Impact' or equivalent as a prerequisite to funding. Getting this right can be crucial to your chances of funding success. Although it goes without saying that to be successful, the research that is proposed must be of the highest quality and novelty, and fit with the aims of the funder. However, many funding panels are faced with a limited pot of money and a choice between a number of proposals that each have the same top-quality rating. In such cases, the quality of your proposed pathway to impact can make the difference between a project being funded or not. Many funding panels include non-academic stakeholders, who may pay particular attention to your knowledge exchange plans, and it may swing a decision in your favour if your impact pathway is particularly credible.

When funded, you need to revisit what you proposed, and update and expand it into a fully-fledged impact plan (sometimes referred to as a knowledge exchange strategy). This will help you to organise, implement and track your knowledge exchange activities and impacts throughout the research process. This will also help with reporting to funders, and if you realise the impacts you set out to achieve, then this process will also help you assess the impact of your research in future years.

What does a top pathway to impact look like?

Funders provide guidance on writing these sections of proposals, but the advice tends to be quite generic, and there are few examples of good practice available. For a recent blog, I therefore asked researchers who had achieved some of the most significant and far-reaching impacts (according to the UK Research Excellence Framework) if they could share with me the sections of their funding proposals that outlined the impacts they were hoping for. Top-scoring (4*) impacts were selected from HEFCE's Research Excellent Framework impact case database and paired for analysis with the sections of the grant proposals that led to them. You can read the full sections of the proposals and the corresponding impact case studies on the Fast Track Impact blog. My colleague Sarah Buckmaster and I analysed the grant proposal texts to identify things they had in common, to derive the following lessons:

1. Clear connectivity from overall vision to objectives and impact
In all the highly rated case studies, the impact planning demonstrated a strong connection from the overall research vision and purpose to the impact objectives and outputs. The take-home message is to make sure there is a story there — a thread running through the whole programme of work. Illustrating this in some way can be helpful to get your team on board and to see how everything fits into the bigger research picture.

2. Tailor-made impact
Pathways to top-scoring impacts didn't just suggest holding meetings or writing policy briefs. They detailed the type of meetings (one-on-one, small group, online, in person), where they'd be held, who would attend — and they did this for each target audience showing that their events were tailor-made for each target market. They detailed the themes and subjects of policy briefings, as well as listing the specific team or individual it would be sent to. You need to take the time to identify and understand your audiences before you can do this, but if you've done that then get creative and tailor-make your impact.

3. Build in flexibility

Although pathways were specific, they also built in flexibility. However, they all demonstrated that having a flexible plan doesn't mean it has to be evasive. You can still be specific within certain phases of the research, for example, collecting evidence in early stages of the research, and then building knowledge exchange and impact around that evidence as it arises.

4. Come up with a plan

Your starting point is the impacts you want to achieve, which you should have identified in the previous step. As part of that process, you have probably already got a fairly good idea of the sorts of individuals, groups and organisations that might benefit from or be interested in that impact.

5. Assign responsibility — name names

All of the successful pathways assigned research team members to specific impact tasks (including monitoring impact) — giving them responsibilities. Seeing specific names on the pathway can often legitimise the work because it shows how people are taking responsibility.

6. Demonstrate demand

Where possible, collect evidence (e.g. market research) that there is a real and pressing need for the impacts you are seeking to generate. For example, if you are creating a web resource, get statistics for the number of visitors to similar types of website.

7. Highlight collaborative partnerships

The successful pathways named specific partnerships that they either already had (and were planning to capitalise on) or that they didn't yet have (but planned to develop). Again, name names and demonstrate an impact plan that is aware of its environment. Develop activities that make use of who and what is already working in the area. If you can collaborate with a partner to create a larger event, then do it. If you can co-produce a textbook with a significant organisation then do it. Partnerships can significantly increase your level of impact, and sometimes decrease the level of staff time.

8. Don't ignore sensitivities

Rather than trying to avoid mentioning any sensitive issues, highlight them to demonstrate the background (market) research and other ground work you have carried out. Mention ethics protocols that will be followed and organisations you will work with to ensure you communicate sensitively with vulnerable groups.

9. Think long term
Demonstrate how you are thinking long term with regards to impact. What will happen at the end of your funded research? Can you describe how what you are putting in place is self-running? Or that you will inspire a group of people who will then manage a process or output?

10. Record everything
This final point isn't specifically for the impact planning, but rather as good practice for every stage of the impact process. All of the most significant and far-reaching impacts had been mindful about capturing impacts throughout the lifetime of the study.

Develop your impact plan

Now you know what a good impact plan looks like, you can start making your own plan. Whether this is a pre-award pathway to impact or you are developing a more detailed plan after having received funding, you will want to go through the following steps.

The first task is to do a stakeholder analysis:
- **Identify who is likely to be interested in your research**, or be able to use or benefit from it in some way
- Next, you can **describe the different motivations, needs and interests of these groups**, and the extent to which you can adapt messages from your research to be relevant to each one
- Then, **consider which stakeholders are likely to have most influence** over your ability to complete the research and generate your intended impacts.

For more information about the importance and benefits of this task, see the second principle (represent, Chapter 3), and for detailed methods and a stakeholder analysis template, see Part 4 of this book.

Once you've identified and analysed your stakeholders, you can **identify activities** that are appropriate to use with different stakeholders to communicate or (if possible) co-produce messages from your research. Tailor these activities to the needs and preferences of each stakeholder, recognising that there may be different sub-groups within any single stakeholder group or organisation who may want to engage in very different ways with you. Pay particular attention to activities you may need to develop for influential and/or hard-to-reach groups, as these may take more time and effort, so you may want to start engaging early with these groups.

Identify indicators or targets that you can use to track whether or not your activities are actually taking you closer to your impact goals. Use this information to adapt or change your activities, so that you ensure you achieve your goals.

Consider the risks associated with achieving your intended impacts, and the activities you have chosen to reach them. What might not work or go wrong? Might there be unintended consequence? How can you mitigate these risks?

Ask what resources or help might you need to achieve your impacts and mitigate these risks. Consider who will be responsible for each activity and when will you time these activities in relation to your research programme and the priorities and agendas of your stakeholder community. Some activities and impacts may be impossible to realise before certain research tasks have been completed. Sometimes it is possible to identify a key date before which preliminary findings could be put to particularly good use (e.g. as part of a policy consultation), and it may be worth considering whether your research schedule could be adapted to provide results in time to be useful for that purpose.

As part of this, make sure you **integrate short-term goals** you identified in the previous step. Some of these might be impact goals in their own right, and some might be indicators or targets that you want to measure your progress towards.

Get others involved in making this plan. Talk to your colleagues and get their feedback, and if you can, get feedback from stakeholders, so that they can tell you if there are particular points at which certain findings could have greater impact. Then make a habit of checking in with these people — make a point of updating yourselves as a research team on your progress towards impact goals as well as updating yourselves on the progress of the research itself. Put it on the agenda of any regular meetings you have with colleagues. And consider how you can create an accountable and collaborative ongoing relationship with the stakeholders who help you make this plan, for example, through a bi-annual stakeholder advisory meeting.

Going public with your aspirations for impact in this way can be powerful for two reasons. First, it holds you to account, and forces you to take yourself and your aspirations seriously. Second, it gives you the opportunity to connect with your team and a bunch of other people who you suddenly discover have similar dreams to you, and can help you. If you work solo without a team, don't skip this step — put your aspirations down in a blog and tweet about it or write about it on Facebook. Or just tell a good friend who you see regularly and ask them if you can keep them updated.

Finally, it is worth noting that there is a danger that impact plans can become too prescriptive. Targets and indicators can help keep your impacts on track, but they shouldn't become a straitjacket that prevents you from adapting your objectives to meet changing stakeholder needs, or exploiting new opportunities as they arise.

Your tasks for this step

1. Do a stakeholder analysis, in which you:
   - Identify who is likely to be interested in your research, or be able to use or benefit from it in some way
   - Identify the different motivations, needs and interests of these groups, and the extent to which you can adapt messages from your research to be relevant to each one
   - Identify which stakeholders are likely to have most influence over your ability to complete the research and generate your intended impacts
2. Identify activities you can use with different stakeholders to communicate or (if possible) co-produce messages from your research. Tailor these activities to the needs and preferences of each stakeholder.
3. Identify indicators or targets that you can use to track whether or not your activities are actually taking you closer to your impact goals.
4. Consider the risks associated with achieving your intended impacts, and the activities you have chosen to reach them. What might not work or go wrong? Might there be unintended consequences? How can you mitigate these risks?
5. Ask what resources or help might you need to achieve your impacts and mitigate these risks.
6. Consider who will be responsible for each activity and when will you time these activities in relation to your research programme and the priorities and agendas of your stakeholder community.

Chapter 10
Step 3: Cut back anything hindering or distracting you from your impact

● ●

Summary

In this step, we will think about how you can make room in your busy schedule for impact-generating activities that are based on trusting relationships with the people who might be interested in and use your research. Relationships take time, and time is in short supply for most researchers, so getting this step right is essential. If you do this step, then it won't just free up time for impact, it will transform your work-life balance too.

● ●

Time is something that is in short supply for most researchers. That's a problem if you want to take a relational approach to impact, because investing in relationships takes time. That's why this step is designed to help you become more efficient and focused as a researcher, so you can make time for relationships with those who are interested in your research (and those other important people in your life, whether or not they are interested in your research!).

Be mindful

Start trying to be mindful of how you spend your time every day, and to what extent each of the things you are doing connect with your impact goals, and your wider life goals. In this step, you are going to identify at least one regular task or activity that you can either entirely cut out of your schedule or drastically cut back on.

Think about how you work with everyone on your team and whether there are people who might benefit from some of the more minor tasks on your to-do list, for example, getting experience reviewing papers that can help them learn how to write more effectively themselves. Consider getting a virtual Personal Assistant (PA). I have a UK-based virtual PA who has experience working with academics, though you can get more generalist virtual PAs who charge less. What would you say if I gave you the choice of a pay rise (say £300 per month) or a whole extra day per week to do whatever you want (you can use it to achieve more in your work or spread your work out over the week so you don't have to work so hard — it's up to you). For most academics, a whole extra day per week is worth much more financially than £300, let alone psychologically. My PA helps me format reference lists, does simple research tasks for me (e.g. how to make a MOOC), writes up notes (including post-it notes and flip-chart paper) from workshops, sets up meetings, organises all my travel and expenses — the list is endless. So next time you get a pay rise, have a think about how you can turn that small amount of extra money into a significant amount of extra time.

Lack of time = lack of priorities

I personally believe that the problem all academics will recognise, of the day never being long enough to do everything we are meant to do, comes down to poor priorities. Lack of time = lack of priorities.

Perhaps you are regularly working evenings and weekends, and don't have time to think (let alone do anything) about generating impacts from your research? I've discovered something interesting over the years, which I've recently found have names: Parkinson's Law and the Pareto Principle.

Parkinson's Law simply recognises that tasks will swell to fill the time you give them. Therefore, you need to limit the time you give to the tasks you need to do. The strange thing is that the end product is usually as good, but is sometimes actually far better, than if you spent double the time on the task. The reason for this, is that the level of focused attention provided by a forced deadline actually enables you to produce more focused work.

I first discovered this in my teaching when I was told I had to head up a research centre, and had significantly less time to prepare my lectures. Without intending to do this, I ended up regularly preparing my lectures on the day of delivery, and although it was more stressful, I was surprised to discover that my ratings from students increased significantly. Admittedly, I had a fairly good grasp of the subjects I was teaching, but the key difference was that I was now having to rely less on my notes and more on my intuition, and as a result my passion for the subject became far more apparent, and this enthusiasm was infectious. I also did more class exercises rather than boring people with information overload, which meant that the students actually learned more. I did the same with a literature review, giving myself just one week to do all the reading and writing of the first draft. It was a hard week's work and I made lots of edits and changes before the final version was eventually published. But this is now by far my most cited paper (>1000 citations) and has played an important role in establishing my reputation in that particular field.

What 20% of your working day produces 80% of the outputs you value most?

The Pareto Principle suggests that for most people, 80% of the outputs you value most come from only 20% of the time you spend working. In reality, it is not exactly 80:20, but I believe that the principle holds for most of us. I think that this principle is the source of many researchers' greatest frustrations and disappointments, because we spend so long every day doing the urgent thing that everyone around us is shouting for at the expense of the less urgent, but far more important things. So that paper or book we dreamed of writing stays unwritten, and we accumulate regret and frustration for the sake of keeping everyone around us happy. I'm not saying that we should stop being team players and be selfish with our time. But if you've got a really important goal in your work, try and spend some time on it every day, even if you only manage half an hour, and you'll be amazed how much more satisfied you feel day after day, week after week. Some people I know get up at five or six in the morning to spend an hour writing or whatever that important task is. I've never been motivated enough to do that, but the point I'm trying to make is that you don't have to spend all day doing the important stuff, but you do have to keep chipping away at it. When you start focusing on the important things, you suddenly realise that many of the urgent things you're being told to do aren't actually that important. With this revelation, it becomes easier to say 'no' or take a few shortcuts to do a 'good enough' job on those tasks, so you can get back to the really important stuff.

So what 20% of your working day produces 80% of the outcomes you value most? Write a list of everything you did yesterday, and if possible estimate how long you spent on it. Be brutally honest about how long you spent replying to emails, on social media and doing other things that yielded very little tangible outcome. For me, this isn't necessarily about cutting these tasks out — you're not going to be popular with your students or colleagues if you stop replying to emails. But it is well worth considering how you could be more strategic.

What could you cut?

Here's a list of the things I have drastically reduced time on, which might inspire you to consider what you could cut:

1. **Social media:** I no longer try and read everything in my feeds, and limit myself to a 20 minute 'news' window every day, where I'm consuming mainstream media via Twitter, a print newspaper to get Scottish news (The National), and the BBC news website. Then, I'm following a targeted social media strategy designed specifically to help me achieve impacts through my research (see Chapter 16 for a guide to writing a social media strategy, and Part 4 for a template you can use to develop your own). Now I'm not blogging into nothingness — I've got a strategy to drive traffic to my most important research outputs and to engage with specific audiences around key messages that link to the impacts I want to achieve.

2. **Email:** I do a scan of the most important and urgent emails in the morning and only reply to these, ignoring the rest till the afternoon, often after lunch when I'm feeling most tired. If necessary, I will send a holding email, acknowledging the email and explaining that I've got a busy morning and that I'll reply later in the day. If I've got a writing deadline (even if it's self-imposed), I will put an out-of-office reply up, explaining that I'm working towards an important deadline and not checking emails for the rest of the week, so please send me a text message if it is urgent, otherwise I'll get back to them as soon as I can.

3. **Reviewing:** none of us can escape this; it is part of our duty to review others' work in as timely and constructive a way as we would hope others would review ours. However, I think we sometimes feel a false sense of duty to review more than we need to. I personally feel that I have met my moral obligation to the academic community if I review around three times as many manuscripts and grant proposals as I submit myself (on the basis that most of the papers and grants I submit will get three reviews each). In addition to only reviewing papers that are in my subject area, I will only review papers from which I think I'm likely to learn something useful or new (based on the abstract). This rule also has a handy way of ensuring you don't end up reviewing papers for predatory journals (if you don't know what these are, look at Beall's List of Predatory Publishers and be careful not to fall prey to these publishers – note that many of the entries on this list are highly contested).

4. **Committee meetings:** there is usually someone absent at each committee meeting you go to, and no one really minds, as long as they aren't always absent. What would happen if you decided to make your apologies for every other committee meeting, citing prior engagements (e.g. you have an urgent writing deadline — whether that deadline is self-imposed or externally imposed is not relevant to your colleagues). What would actually happen? Would the committee cease to function? If you missed out on a key piece of information or decision, would there be no other way to find this out or influence that decision? Obviously it is wise to check the agenda and if you're chairing the committee then this won't be possible, but if you're not chairing it, do you really have to be at every single one?

5. **Chat:** it is incredible how much time is wasted, just chatting in the corridors, or with people randomly passing your office

door who want to say 'hello'. Rather than leaving your office door open with an invitation to be interrupted, make yourself fully available to anyone by appointment, and then stack all your appointments into a single day or a couple of days in the week. This doesn't mean that you need to become a hermit and avoid all social contact, but now you can be strategic and targeted in who you actually invest time with, whether professionally or as friends, by taking these people for coffee or lunch, where you can have quality time together. Since my PhD, I have always worked primarily from home, coming into the department on selected days, for meetings and to socialise. The rest of the week is for being productive and focused.

Those are just a few of the things I've done over the years to increase my productivity. I'm not suggesting you should cut back in the same areas, but hopefully this list gives you a flavour of the sorts of things that might be possible.

Do less to do more

I think that many of us think somehow that the world will end if we stop doing some of the things that all other academics do. But stop and ask yourself the question: what will actually happen if I stop doing this? Really? Think of your worst-case scenario, and then consider if you could reverse, cope with or recover from that situation. If you'd manage to cope with the worst-case scenario, then go ahead and cut it. In almost every case, that worst-case will never actually come to pass.

We all know that there will always be many more things that we 'ought' to be doing every day, which we run out of time for. The art of being a successful academic with some semblance of work-life balance,is more about what you choose not to do, rather than what you do. The more time you give to your work, the more tasks will fill up that time. That's why since my PhD I made the decision to never work weekends, and only to work evenings when I or my wife was travelling. I feel rested and refreshed on a Monday morning and I don't resent my work. That simple act of constraining my time is, I believe, one of the reasons I have been able to be so productive.

My message is this: do less to do more. Limit your tasks to only the most important, so that you shorten the amount of time you have to work. Then, shorten the amount of time you have to work, so that you are forced to limit your tasks to only the most important.

Tasks for this step

1. Make a list of everything you did during your work day yesterday (or your last typical day in the office), and how long you spent on each task, including menial and non-work tasks during the work day.
2. Commit today to removing one thing from your schedule to make room for impact-generating activities. If you can, commit to removing as many other things as you can, so that in addition to being more productive, you can get a better work-life balance (which of course, will make you more productive in the hours you do work).

Chapter 11
Step 4: Get specific about your impacts and the people who can help you

Summary

Your task in this step is to come up with one thing you can do this month that will take you closer to achieving impact. In parallel with this, and to help you actually do this one thing, you will identify key individuals who can help you achieve the impacts you want to see.

Now you have cut back anything that might be hindering or distracting you from your impact (Step 3, Chapter 10), you can revisit your impact plan (Step 2, Chapter 9) and start to get specific about the impact and activities you want to prioritise for action this month.

Whose footsteps are you following in?

Being successful at something is much easier when you are surrounded by other people who are already being successful at that task. Being connected to other people who are on the same journey towards impact as you, who already have some experience under their belt, means you can call on each other for help and advice. It is also motivating to see what others have done, and to see how they achieved these successes.

These people will probably be other academics, but they may be knowledge brokers from NGOs, industry or elsewhere. They may already be achieving some of the sorts of impacts that you would like to be able to achieve yourself.

What they will have in common is that they are a few steps ahead of you on their pathways to impact. They may be ahead of you in terms of their experience generating impacts generally, or specifically generating a particular type of impact or using a particular technique, technology or activity that you would like to be able to use yourself.

It is surprising how open many people are to being contacted by someone who wants to learn from them. If this is done in a spirit of humility, most people will respond positively and be willing to mentor you in some shape or form. Even as a PhD student, I reached out to key authors in my field to co-author papers as part of my PhD, and got incredible mentoring from these researchers in addition to the inputs of my PhD supervisor (and ended up publishing 12 papers out of my PhD, six of which have been cited over 100 times). So don't be shy!

Create your influence network

In a moment, I'm going to ask you to identify five people who are a few steps ahead of you on their pathway to impact, who might be able to mentor you. Next, I'd like you to identify five more people. This time, rather than looking for mentors, I'd like you to look for influential

stakeholders who might have the power to enable you to have significant impact. They may have knowledge and contacts that could significantly help you to achieve your goals. They might have resources at their disposal that they want to use to achieve similar goals to yours. They might have significant followings on social media that could enable you to get your message across to a wide audience. They might have access to data, hard-to-reach groups or sites that you need to complete your research. You might already have identified some of these people in your stakeholder analysis in Step 2 (it is worth going back and looking at the groups you identified as being particularly influential). These people are worth their weight in gold, so it is a good idea to spend time talking with colleagues and trying your best to identify these individuals, so you can begin to connect with and draw upon their influence to help you achieve your impacts.

Tasks for this step

1. Identify one impact you could work on this month. This could be your most important impact, identified in Step 2, the goal you identified in Step 1 that you could do in the next six months, or it could be another impact, but ideally it should link in some way to your most important impact. Then identify a specific activity that will help you achieve that impact (even if it is only the first of many steps you will have to take to reach the impact).

2. Make a list of five people who you feel are ahead of you in achieving impact or working with the end users of research — these people will probably be other academics, but they may be knowledge brokers from NGOs, industry or elsewhere.

3. Make a list of five stakeholders from Step 2 who are likely to be particularly influential in enabling you to complete your research successfully and make an impact.

4. Make a commitment to reach out to at least one person from each list this month to try and establish a working relationship that can help you achieve impacts from your research. Prioritise those who might be able to help with the one thing you've decided.

Chapter 12
Step 5: Achieve your first step towards impact and monitor your success

∎∎

Summary

In this final step, you will take your first step towards achieving impact and start monitoring your success. This isn't about achieving your impact now (though in some cases this may be possible), but about taking purposeful, measurable steps each day that take you closer to specific impacts you are targeting. Focus on small steps every day and celebrate your progress.

∎∎

If you have completed the tasks at the end of each of the preceding steps, then you have already invested wisely in yourself and are a huge step closer to being able to generate significant and far-reaching impacts from your research. You now have a much clearer idea of the impacts you want to achieve and why you want to achieve them. You've got a clear plan that can get you from where you are now to the impacts you want to see in the future. You've cut back on the things that have been cluttering, confusing and holding you back to make more time for yourself and more time to generate impact. And you've identified a network of people who can help you reach your goals.

During the last step, you identified one thing you could work on this month, which could take you closer to achieving impact. During this step, you will actually start work on this. It is important that you actually do something tangible as part of this step. You've done a lot of thinking, discussing and planning so far, but taken little real action. Now is the time to put everything you have learned into practice.

Put theory into practice

In the last step, you identified one thing you could work on this month. If it isn't particularly tangible, then your first task is to find a way to make it more tangible. Is there a way you could involve others to do this with you, for example, in a workshop setting with stakeholders? Is there some sort of physical artefact that you could produce, linked to the thing you've decided to work on, like a policy brief, a film or an educational resource?

Next, go back to your impact plan in Step 2, and think as deeply as you can about the activities you will do, how they link to your impact, how you can adapt your activities to the needs of different stakeholders, and the risks that might be associated with those activities. If you haven't already, get some feedback from colleagues about what you are planning to do, to see if they can spot any flaws or limitations in your plan.

Next go to the people you reached out to in Step 4 — they should already be waiting for your email or call, if you set this up right when you contacted them. Although it might feel uncomfortable at first, your task is to ask them for help. Ask for something very specific, that you think they should in theory be able to give you. If you don't ask, you will never know if they would have been happy to help you, and more often than not, people actually want to help.

Finally, just go out and do it — whatever the thing is that you decided to do, and make sure you do it within four weeks, so that you can maintain momentum.

Double your failure rate

There is one last thing you need to consider though. It probably feels great that you are actually out there, doing something tangible to generate impact. But how do you know that what you have done has actually effected change, and helped you get closer to your impact? In the impact plan I mentioned in Step 2 (see the template in Part 4), there's a column where you have to identify indicators or targets. Make sure that you design whatever it is that you do this month, so that there is some way of collecting information about whether or not it is working. If it didn't work as well as you wanted, do something else next month. Those who succeed most in life are often those who are prepared to experience failure again and again, and it is for this very reason that they learn how to succeed. As the American businessman and philanthropist Thomas Watson Jnr put it: "if you want to increase your success rate, double your failure rate".

For many of us, this requires a very different perception of failures, not as things to be avoided at all costs, but rather as inevitable twists on the road to success, from which we can learn important lessons. Learning to accept and embrace failure takes a degree of self-confidence that I only achieve on good days. I think that one of the reasons that failure is so hard to accept as a researcher is the level of personal creativity we invest in our work, and the fact that we are our own brand with a reputation that is inextricably linked to our name. For this reason, it is difficult not to take professional rejection personally. However, this can be the beginning of a downward spiral. The most common cause of writers block among colleagues I've been asked to mentor is lack of confidence. And my own periods without research funding have been prolonged by self-doubt that anything I could ever submit would be fundable. Before you can complete a sentence of your paper or proposal, you can hear the critiques of the reviewers ringing in your ears.

The trick, I believe, is not to ignore those voices but to embrace them, and tackle each critique constructively as it comes to mind. When you call these critiques to mind consciously and make them explicit, you can start to distinguish between genuine insights about weaknesses in your work (which you can address) and the inner psycho-babble that (in my case) tells you you're worthless and can't do it (which you can also address, but in different ways). Rather than hearing these critiques as criticism and allowing them to cripple you with low self-esteem, work hard on turning these internal voices into something that can propel you forward. I think it is hardest when you know you messed up. With hindsight, you can see what mistakes you made that led to failure. However, it is still possible to learn from these mistakes, if you don't take your failures personally and pick yourself up and try again. Andrew Derrington, in *The Research Funding Toolkit*, tries to help by conceiving of research as a "grants factory", in which researchers churn out proposals dispassionately on a production line, starting work on the next proposal as soon as the last

one is submitted, and accepting the odds that if your work is any good, then eventually one will get funded. Whether or not you are able to detach yourself from your work to that extent (I'm not sure I can), I think that there is something to be said for just picking yourself up and carrying on, no matter how bad your failure.

I've experienced a number of talks in which I "went down in flames" — usually as a result of my own lack of preparation rather than any killer question. I think the most acutely embarrassing was a particularly high-profile conference that I'd been told I had to present at by my funders. I knew that I had to find and impress the head of the Commission for Rural Communities, as he was commissioning work for an inquiry that would influence policy. The great and the good, including the head of the organisation that had funded my research, were sitting in the front row, and I was nervous. I finished my talk about UK uplands, and the head of the Commission stood up to ask the first question. As I tried to make a mental note of what he looked like, so I could find him later, the pressure suddenly became too much for me. He had asked the most ridiculously easy question, and it was the simplicity of the question that put so much pressure on me; I knew that a strong answer to his question would easily convince him that we should do the work for his inquiry. But my mind went completely blank. I could think of nothing — absolutely nothing — to say. Sir Howard Newby, then head of the Higher Education Funding Council for England was chairing the session, and politely looked at me and said into his microphone, "I think this one is for you Mark". All I could say was, "I know". After what felt like an age, Sir Howard took another question and someone else on the panel of speakers answered, while I wished I could magically disappear. To make matters worse, I thought I could redeem myself by asking an intelligent-sounding question of the speaker who followed me. I finished my question, feeling like I might have regained a tiny amount of credibility with the audience, and Sir Howard intervened, saying "You do realise that the legislation you're asking about applies only to uplands, and this research is all about lowlands, don't you?". I could have died of embarrassment as my fellow speaker came to my rescue with an answer to my unanswerable question.

We've all been there. Everyone has got stories like this, that we don't typically tell (let alone write about in books), and because we don't tell our failure stories, we end up with this perception that we are the only people who fail, and everyone else moves from one success story to the next. I think we need to be brave enough to start laughing about our failures so we can all learn from each others' mistakes and move forward together more empathetically to achieve impact, no matter how many failures it takes along the road.

Focus on the small steps that take you closer to impact every day

Make it your goal to take small steps every day that you believe will contribute to your impact. At the heart of this book is a relational philosophy of impact, which focuses on building empathic, trusting and respectful relationships. Make a mental note of all the small things you did each day that were consistent with applying this philosophy, whether or not it is obvious how it helped you get closer to impact.

Focus on repeating value-orientated behaviours again and again, and trust that these will take you where you need to go. This doesn't mean you don't monitor and correct your course — but rather than focusing on whether you've reached the top of the mountain yet, celebrate that you took a few more steps that were in the right direction that day.

Finally, if you have evidence that your activities are working, or even better, that you are actually achieving impacts, then shout about it! Celebrate and share your success with others who are on a similar journey to you, so they can be inspired and learn from you.

Tasks for this step

1. Start working on the impact you identified in the previous step — make it tangible and actually do something. Now is not the time for planning or talking about it. Now is the time to actually put your impact plan into action.
2. Reach out to the people you connected with in the previous step and ask them to help you achieve this impact with you this month.
3. Make sure you collect information that can tell you whether or not your activities are actually taking you closer to impact.
4. Make sure you've got a network of others who can support and help each other as you all achieve impacts over the long term.
5. If you want extra help with all five steps, you can sign up to receive each step via email every week over five weeks on the Fast Track Impact website. I'll talk you through each step in a short video, and I'll give you personal help with your ideas for impact.

Part 3: Tools and techniques

Chapter 13
How to work out who is interested in your research: stakeholder analysis

If you want to understand who is likely to be interested in your research, and who is likely to want to use your findings, then you need to invest a bit of time thinking about this systematically. Depending on the type of research you are doing, and the sorts of impact you want to achieve, you will need to identify stakeholders or publics (or both).

Segmenting publics

For less applied research disciplines and topics, there is no identifiable 'use' of your research, but that shouldn't stop you trying to use your research to make a difference. Whether you are working on astrophysics or 18th-century romantic literature, it is possible to find audiences who are interested in aspects of your work, whose lives you can enrich through engagement. There are many good resources available about how to do audience segmentation (see the National Co-ordinating Centre on Public Engagement www.publicengagement.ac.uk for an overview and resources). This section provides an overview.

The first step in segmenting publics is to identify groups of people who share characteristics that are likely to make them more interested in your research, for example, using research on feminist literature to empower women through writing groups, and working with groups interested in the outdoors (such as walkers and cyclists) to raise awareness about threats to the landscapes they are enjoying. In this context, social marketing techniques are particularly relevant, where messages based on research are tailored to the interests of different audiences to 'nudge' them towards changing attitudes and behaviours. In well-funded projects, this would normally start with work that is designed to understand the attitudes and behaviours of different groups in relation to the research area, for example, family planning or sustainable living. Then different messages are developed that are likely to be acceptable and attractive to those different groups.

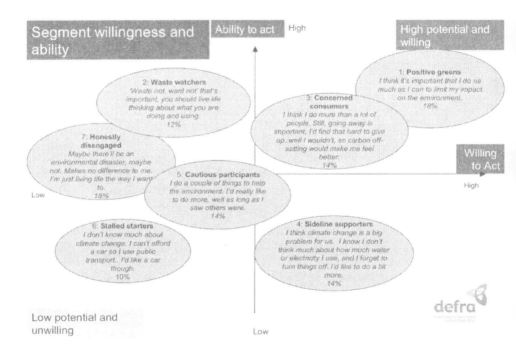

Figure 4: Defra's segmentation model divides the public into seven clusters, each sharing a distinct set of attitudes and beliefs towards the environment, environmental issues and behaviours, based on responses to a broad range of attitudinal questions as part of the 2007 Defra attitudes and behaviours survey (source: Defra (2008). A framework for pro-environmental behaviours. HMSO, London).

The problem with this is that most research can only be communicated in a fairly limited number of ways, and there are only so many ways you can adapt messages from your research whilst remaining true to your findings. For example, messages around research on new family planning techniques could not be adapted to suit the attitudes of groups who oppose family planning on religious or moral grounds. On the other hand, during my research on peatlands, I've managed to adapt messages from this work to emphasise benefits for conservation, the economy and farming communities, depending on the interests of the different groups I've been working with. For me, there is nothing disingenuous about this. I am just emphasising certain aspects of the research. I am not hiding the other aspects or manipulating the findings to suit the audience. However, not everyone feels comfortable with this approach.

To illustrate how this can look, Figure 4 shows how the UK government's Department for Environment, Food and Rural Affairs segmented the public in relation to attitudes towards climate change, to help them develop messages based on the latest research evidence that would be most likely to change each group's behaviour to adopt more pro-environmental behaviours.

Whether you're focusing on specific stakeholders or wider publics, the key point that I want to make under this principle, is the need to identify those who are most likely to be interested in or use your research. It can sometimes be quite intimidating to discover just how many different groups and organisations might be interested in your work. There is never going to be enough time for most researchers to contact, let alone meaningfully engage with, all these people. However, by analysing your stakeholders and segmenting your publics, you can start to prioritise who you engage with first, and, most importantly, how you engage with them. If you can represent each group's interests, needs and priorities when you engage with them, you are likely to save yourself (and them) a lot of time, and engage in ways that are useful for everyone involved.

Methods for stakeholder analysis

For more applied research, stakeholder analysis is a powerful tool for identifying and prioritising stakeholders for engagement, so you use your time efficiently and effectively. A good stakeholder analysis forms the basis for any good impact plan, so it is worth investing time in this.

The most commonly used approach is to consider the relative interest of a stakeholder in the issue or decision being considered versus their level of influence over that issue or decision. This is typically done using an 'interest-influence matrix' (Figures 6 and 7). Using this approach, you can classify stakeholders as key players, context setters, subjects and the crowd (Box 8).

Although by far the most commonly used stakeholder mapping tool, interest-influence matrices are rather simplistic, I think, as there are many other factors that might usefully inform the categorisation and prioritisation of stakeholders. For this reason, I use an **extendable matrix** that considers levels of interest and influence (see Chapter 13 for detailed methods and the stakeholder analysis template and example in Part 4 of this book). However, these matrices also attempt to characterise the *nature* of those interests and give people the opportunity to document reasons for the level of influence that is ascribed (e.g. considering whether a stakeholder holds more or less influence in different contexts or at different times).

Such matrices can then be extended to consider a range of other factors that may help categorise and engage effectively with stakeholders, for example, identifying any important relationships between stakeholders (e.g. coalitions or conflicts), information about how best to approach and engage with different stakeholders, and contact information that can be used to check and further extend the analysis.

For most researchers, considering relationships between stakeholders in a column of the extendable matrix is enough to identify the most important conflicts and alliances. If you have time and resources, and are interested in knowing more about the social context you are going to be working in, there are a range of other methods that have been developed to understand relationships between stakeholders. These include methods to analyse the structure of social networks, to map stakeholder perceptions and values, and methods to assess and analyse conflicts between stakeholders (e.g. Figure 8). Although these relationships may be used to categorise and prioritise stakeholders for engagement, these sorts of analyses are typically conducted after stakeholders have been categorised, to understand how different stakeholder groups interact with one another, and to identify specific individuals or organisations that may play an important role in diffusing knowledge or practices within and between different groups of stakeholders. Such methods can be useful to identify opportunities and risks of engaging with certain stakeholders, and identify the values and priorities of different groups, so that these can be taken into account in the design of an impact plan.

Finally, it should be noted that all methods for identifying stakeholders provide a snapshot in time, and stakeholders and their interests and influence are typically dynamic. For example, stakeholders may form alliances to either promote or defeat a particular outcome and stakeholder mapping can be used to identify where such alliances are likely to arise. This requires stakeholder mapping exercises to be revisited and updated periodically to ensure that the needs and priorities of all stakeholders continue to be captured.

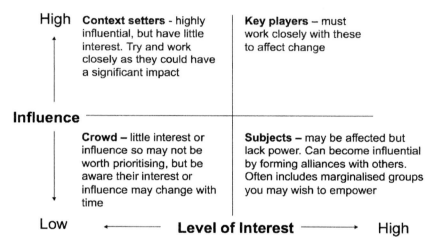

Figure 6: Interest-influence matrix used to identify stakeholders with differing levels of interest in and influence over your research

Box 8: Categories of stakeholder in an interest-influence matrix

- Stakeholders with high levels of interest and influence are termed **key players**, and it is argued by some that priority should be given to engaging actively with this group.
- **Context setters** are highly influential, but have little interest in your research. For example, your work may be marginal to their interest, or be perceived as a narrow and hence minor angle on a bigger issue. Because of their influence, they may have significant influence over the success of your research, but may be difficult to engage with. As such, particular effort may be necessary to engage this group in the research.
- **Subjects** have high levels of interest in your research but low levels of influence and although by definition they are supportive, they are unlikely to be able to play a significant role in implementing findings from your research. They may, however, later become influential by forming alliances with other more influential stakeholders. These are often the marginal stakeholders that may also be considered "hard to reach", and that might warrant special attention to secure their engagement and to empower them to engage as equals in your research with more influential participants. However, the low level of influence held by this group is often used as a justification for excluding them from the research process
- The **crowd** are stakeholders who have little interest in or influence over your research and its desired outcomes and there is little need to consider them in much detail or to engage with them.

116

A quick and easy method of stakeholder analysis that captures everything you need to know

I would recommend that you invite a small number of non-academics who know the stakeholder landscape well to help you with this task. But if you are short on time, then even if you just fill out the template in Part 4 with your research team, you will be able to do far more impactful research than you would have done if you did not take this step.

The following methodology will take you approximately two days to complete, including between half a day and a day for an initial workshop (see the example facilitation plan in Part 4), followed by a series of half-hour telephone interviews to check your findings with key stakeholders (which is also a great opportunity to get their feedback on the focus of your research and start getting ownership as you adapt your work to stakeholder interests). The following steps are designed to be straightforward and replicable, but this does not mean that they should be inflexibly applied. Local circumstances may require these steps to be adapted, to ensure that the stakeholder analysis is a tool that brings stakeholders together and facilitates active engagement in research.

1. **Identify cross-cutting stakeholders:** Identify between two and four individuals from cross-cutting stakeholder organisations who operate at the scale of your research (if you have multiple study sites, you may need to do this for each site). The key criterion for selection is their breadth of interest in the issues you are researching, so that they are familiar with the widest possible range of organisations that might have a stake in your work. Aim to represent a range of different perspectives on the issue, so that you can facilitate debate about the relative interest and influence of different stakeholders (e.g. someone from a government department or agency and someone from an NGO, not just people from different government departments).

2. **Invite cross-cutting stakeholders to a half-day workshop:** only two to four stakeholders plus project team should be present, as it is not the aim to represent all stakeholders at this workshop (this isn't possible as we have yet to systematically identify them). This workshop should take approximately four hours (half a day), but if there is time, it is more relaxed to do this over a day:

a) **Clearly establish the focus of the research that you think individuals, organisations or groups might have a stake in:** it is important to be as specific as possible about your focus, so you can clearly identify who has a stake and who does not. You might want to consider the geographical or sectoral scope of the project (e.g. are you interested only in stakeholders at a local level, or is this a national issue that may involve national or international stakeholders?). Which sectors of the economy or population are relevant to the research? A discussion about these sorts of questions at the start of the workshop should clarify any differing perceptions amongst the group, to avoid confusion later

b) Choose a well-known stakeholder organisation and **run through the stakeholder analysis for this organisation as an example.** Draw copies of the extendable matrix in Part 4 on flip-chart paper and stick to walls, so that everyone can see what is being done. Explain that interest and influence can be both positive and negative (e.g. a group's interests might be negatively affected and they may have influence to block as well as facilitate)

c) Ask participants to **identify organisations, groups or individuals that are particularly interested and/or influential**, and list them in the first column of the matrix in Part 4. I've provided you with a blank table and a worked example to illustrate how this might look. Use the questions in the box below as prompts to help you identify as many stakeholders as possible

d) As a group, **work through each of the columns in the matrix**, one stakeholder at a time, discussing the nature of their interest and reasons for their influence etc., and capturing the discussion as best as possible in the matrix (getting participants to capture points on post-it notes where necessary to avoid taking too long)

e) Take a break, and then invite participants to use the remaining time working individually to **complete the columns for all the remaining stakeholders**, adding rows for less interested and influential stakeholders as they go. Remind people to try and identify groups who might typically be marginalised or disadvantaged, but who still have strong interest in the research

f) **Ask participants to check** the work done by other participants, adding their own comments with post-it notes where they disagree or don't understand

g) **Facilitate a discussion of key points** people feel should be discussed as a group about stakeholders where there is particular disagreement or confusion and resolve these where possible (accepting differing views where it is not possible to resolve differences)

h) **Identify key individuals to check findings with after the workshop.** Identify up to five individuals from particularly influential organisations, trying to get as wide a spread of different interests as possible (to do this, it may be necessary to start with a longer list and then identify people who are likely to provide similar views to reduce the length of the list). Finally, consider if there are any particularly important stakeholders who have high levels of interest but low influence, who you do not want to marginalise and go through the same process, to arrive at a list of around seven to eight individuals who you can check the findings of the workshop with.

Box 9 provides some questions and example categories that may help you identify stakeholders. You can photocopy the table in Part 4 of this book to use a template for your own stakeholder analysis. Feel free to change the titles of the columns, as I've done in the worked example at the end of this chapter (just make sure you still capture the interest and influence of each stakeholder, and be aware that the more columns you have, the longer it will take to complete).

Box 9: Useful prompts to help identify stakeholders

A number of questions may be asked during workshops and interviews to identify stakeholders, for example:
- Who will be affected by the research?
- Will the impacts be local, national or international?
- Who has the power to influence the outcomes of the research?
- Who are potential allies and opponents?
- What coalitions might build around the issues being researched?
- Are there people whose voices or interests in the issue may not be heard?
- Who will be responsible for managing the outcome?
- Who can facilitate or impede the outcome through their participation, non-participation or opposition?
- Who can contribute financial or technical resources towards the research?

Example stakeholder categories include:
- Government departments and politicians
- Government agencies
- Industry/producer representative bodies/associations
- Media
- Trading partners
- Land owners and managers
- Special interest/lobby groups
- National representative and advisory groups
- Research organisations
- Professional groups and their representative bodies
- Representative groups e.g. for consumers or patients
- NGOs
- Community groups
- Local history groups
- Museum curators and staff
- Schools

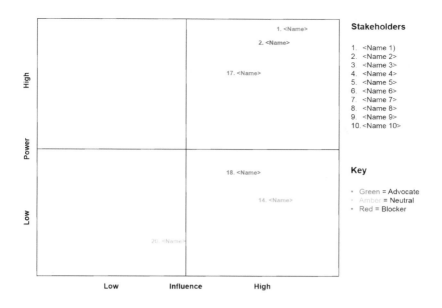

Figure 7: Example of an interest-influence matrix from www.pmmajik.com

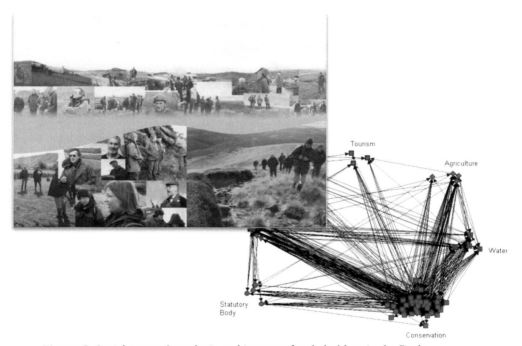

Figure 8: Social network analysis and images of stakeholders in the Peak District National Park (red dots represent individuals, grouped according to their interests, and arrows connect individuals who communicate with each other)

121

Chapter 14
How to design events with stakeholders and members of the public

The chances are that your pursuit of impact is likely to involve talking to more than one stakeholder at a time, and that these individuals may have quite differing perspectives. For many researchers, the prospect of having to negotiate and potentially mediate between conflicting parties is their worst nightmare. The good news is that even with the most challenging of groups, you can almost completely design conflict (and boredom) out of your meeting. There is no substitute for working with a professional facilitator to design and facilitate your workshop, but if you don't have the budget or time to hire someone, these suggestions will go a long way towards helping you design an event that delivers what everyone wants and is efficient and enjoyable.

A conceptual model for designing your event

The GROW model comes from the coaching literature and offers a useful conceptual framework within which to think about planning events. It suggests that we need to start by considering the goals of the event, then consider how far the current situation is from the goals you want to achieve, before considering options to get you from where you are now to your goal, and deciding on actions. Although this may sound like common sense, the questions in Box 10 can be a powerful way of checking that your event is action-orientated, and contributes towards the goals of your research.

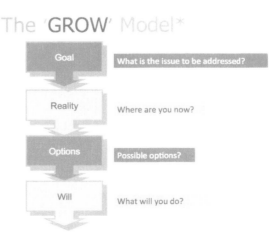

The 'GROW' Model*

Goal — What is the issue to be addressed?

Reality — Where are you now?

Options — Possible options?

Will — What will you do?

Box 10: Structuring a process, event or group conversation with GROW

First, think about the **goals** you have set for working with stakeholders and likely users of your research:
- What do you want to achieve together or change?
- How will you know if you've been successful?
- When do you want to have achieved your goal?

Next, consider your current **reality**:
- What stage are you at in your research?
- What are you achieving at present in your research in relation to the goals you want to achieve?
- What action have you taken so far to try and reach your goals? What were the effects of this action?

Next, consider your **options**:
- What actions could you take to move forward?
- What strategies have worked before in similar circumstances?
- If no barriers or limitations existed, what would you do?
- Which step will give the best result?
- Advantages/disadvantages of this step?
- Which option will you work on first?

Finally, consider what you **will** do now, at the end of this workshop or meeting with stakeholders:
- What are you going to do?
- When are you going to do it?
- What help do you need?
- Who will you involve?
- What might prevent you from taking this step?
- How can you overcome this?

You can also use this model to structure the overall process within which your event will sit (e.g. a series of meetings and events or activities), and it can be used to structure open discussion during events to ensure it is action orientated, and not a talking shop.

Process design

Before considering how to design a specific event, it is important to consider the context in which that event sits. There are two elements to this: the context in which your stakeholders are operating; and your research context. If you have followed the second step in this book, based on the second principle (represent), you should know who is likely to be interested in your research, and what their interests are. You can then ask the following questions to help you design a process that helps you achieve impact from your research whilst meeting stakeholder needs:

- What outcomes do you want from the event?
- What are the outcomes that stakeholders and likely users of your research want (based on your stakeholder analysis)?
- Where are the areas of overlap and synergy between your goals and the goals that you think stakeholders are likely to bring to your process? Can you emphasise and focus primarily on these?
- Are there any outcomes you want that stakeholders are likely to oppose, or that stakeholders want and you would not feel comfortable with or able to help deliver? Can you design additional meetings and workshops to negotiate goals with key stakeholders to avoid these clashing interests?
- How does your planned event link to the wider research project, and your funder's and organisation's goals? Can you combine or link your event with another event to make your process more efficient?
- How will you attract people to engage with your event?
- How will you keep people engaged with your research after your event?
- What steps will you need to put in place after your event to ensure you achieve your intended impacts?

Armed with the answers to these questions, you can now develop a process plan in which you organise a range of meetings, events or other activities around your event to ensure you achieve the impacts you want. Decide how many events of which type you need with which groups of stakeholders, and integrate this with your impact plan.

Event design

If you want an event to run smoothly, there are a large number of things you need to do beforehand. There are many important practicalities that are frequently overlooked by researchers when designing events. All it takes is for your venue to tell you that you're not allowed to stick anything up on the walls (as has happened to me on a number of occasions) and suddenly your event plan is in tatters if all your activities involved people writing on posters on the wall. So pay attention to these practicalities to avoid last minute stress:

- How many people do you expect to attend your event? Is your room sufficiently large to accommodate everyone, with extra room for people to move around to do group activities or contribute to material being developed on the walls of the room?
- With larger groups, it can be useful to split into smaller groups for certain activities to ensure everyone has a chance to discuss issues in depth:
  - Do you need to book break-out rooms or will the room be large enough for small groups to be able to work separately around the room without disturbing each other?
  - Do you want small groups to be facilitated or self-facilitating? Getting groups to nominate a facilitator to help steer discussion and capture notes may be efficient, but if they are facilitating properly, it means that you're unable to fully capture the views of that member of the group. Often naturally more dominant group members may offer to facilitate and then abuse this position by not allowing others to talk or not fully capturing their points in the notes that are developed. This can lead to frustration amongst group members and biased outcomes. Therefore, although more costly and time-consuming, it may be worth assigning a facilitator to each group. Alternatively, to reduce costs, you can approach individuals you think might be effective facilitators in advance and ask them to arrive early to get guidance on good practice facilitation

- For research projects operating in controversial areas or where there is conflict between stakeholders, you may need to take care to ensure the venue is considered 'neutral' territory. For example, don't accept a free room from a controversial organisation on one side of a conflict
- Consider how your choice of venue might influence power dynamics among the group you are inviting, for example, might hosting your event at the university intimidate some participants and increase discrepancies in power between those with more or less formal educational status?

- If you are planning to use facilitation techniques that involve putting flip-chart paper on walls, ensure that you have sought permission to do this, as some venues forbid you from sticking things on the walls. Even if you think a flip-chart stand will be sufficient, it is often useful to have the flexibility to be able to put things on the wall, so participants can see a record of what has been discussed so far, and build on it in subsequent tasks
- Is the venue able to provide lunch to participants in a timely manner? Booking a sit-down lunch can lead to unexpected delays, extending your lunch break and taking up valuable workshop time. A buffet lunch may give you the option to reduce time for the lunch break and act as a useful buffer if you're running behind schedule
- Is the venue fully accessible to everyone you've invited — consider both distance and other accessibility issues, such as whether it is accessible via wheelchairs and public transport
- Have you booked your event at an appropriate time for your target audience? Weekdays will be better for some types of participant, while evenings or weekends may be better for others — you may have to devise two similar events to reach different audiences. Consider the time of year you've booked your event — might winter weather prevent some people from reaching you if you choose a remote location? Are there other key events happening the same day? Is it a particularly busy time of year for some of the professions you're targeting (tax returns due or farmers in lambing season)?
- Do you have all the equipment you're likely to need to carry out your facilitation plan (see below for more information about how to develop an effective facilitation plan)? Even if not part of your facilitation plan, it can be useful to travel with post-it notes and sticky dots, in case you need to give everyone the opportunity to write down their thoughts on a particular issue, or if you need to rank or prioritise anything by getting people to stick dots next to ideas they prefer (more anonymous and easier to record than voting)

Developing an event (facilitation) plan

A facilitation plan is a bit like a detailed recipe for your workshop, that should be self-explanatory and easy to understand for everyone who is helping you facilitate (including you when you're stressed!). Although this may be based around an agenda with timings that match the items on the participants' agenda, it will need to be significantly expanded to provide more details to help you manage the day. A good facilitation plan should include these things:

- **Assign a time-keeper** from the team to keep an eye on timings and remind others in your facilitation team when it is time to move on. Provide detailed timings for each agenda item — if you need to do a number of activities to achieve a particular agenda item, list each of these activities and estimate timings. Consider removing timings (or keeping them to a minimum) on the participants' agenda, to avoid people noticing if you're running late, so you can easily adapt the programme to catch up time without people worrying they'll be going home late or missing lunch

- **Assign members of your facilitation team to each activity** in your facilitation plan. Where possible, include a lead and a support facilitator — the support facilitator can help record points, get extra materials when they run out and generally help keep everything running smoothly so that the lead facilitator can focus on the participants

- **Set clear aims** for your event, and then tailor your techniques to the aims and the interests/needs of participants. For details of techniques you may wish to choose from, keep reading

- **Make time for introductions** at the start of your event (unless the group size is too large for this) and create time at the end of the day after participants have left for your facilitation team to debrief

- To ensure your event leads to some practical outcomes, it is worth programming in an **action planning** session at the end of your event where you identify actions that have arisen as a result of your workshop, so you can assign deadlines and responsibilities and follow these up later

- It can be useful to **start your event with 'opening out and exploring' techniques, followed by 'analysing' and then 'closing down and deciding' techniques** to structure your dialogue as inclusively as possible towards a practical outcome (Box 11)

- It is useful to **include a 'buffer' session in your timings**, such as a long lunch that can be cut short if necessary, or a session that could be cut out if time is running short. This will prevent people feeling rushed, and allow you to spend enough time on the important aspects of the workshop. I usually identify a session in the afternoon that could be significantly shortened or completely removed without significantly compromising the workshop, in case I'm running short on time or need to create time for a new session in response to a problem
- **Create an equipment list**, making sure you have all the equipment you need for every activity (don't assume the venue will have anything you can use to stick paper on walls)
- **Trial and test your methods.** If you've not tried a particular facilitation technique/method before, its never a good idea to try things out for the first time with stakeholders — try and use it in a research meeting or in class with students first, to check you know how it works properly and adapt it accordingly

Engagement techniques

There are many techniques available to facilitate two-way engagement between researchers and stakeholders as part of the research process (Box 11). I typically start a workshop with opening up and exploratory techniques, before moving on to analysing and deciding techniques. However, you may want to have a separate workshop at the start of your research that is focused entirely on opening up and exploring, to understand the research priorities of your stakeholders and adapt your research accordingly. Below I've listed some of the techniques I use most often in my own research. Having these in your mind can be incredibly useful if a technique isn't working for some reason and you need a Plan B.

Box 11: Types of engagement technique

- **Opening up and exploring** dialogue and gathering information with stakeholders about issues linked to your research (goals in the GROW model)
- **Analysing** issues in greater depth with stakeholders, getting feedback on preliminary findings (reality and then options in GROW)
- **Closing down and deciding** on options and actions based on research findings (will in the GROW model)

Opening up and exploratory techniques include, for example:

- **Brainstorming** techniques can help rapidly identify initial ideas from a group. By getting participants to think rapidly and express their ideas in short phrases, the technique encourages participants to suspend the normal criteria they would use to filter out ideas that may not appear immediately relevant or acceptable. As such, many of the ideas may not be useable, but there may be a number of new and creative ideas that would not have been expressed otherwise, that can be further developed later in an event.
- In a **metaplan,** participants are given a fixed number of post-it notes (usually between two and five depending on the size of the group, with fewer post-its being given out in larger groups), and are asked to write one idea per post-it. Participants then take their post-its and place them on flip-chart paper on the wall, grouping identical, similar or linked ideas together. The facilitator then summarises each group, checks the participants are happy with the grouping (making changes where necessary) and circles and names each group. In the space of 10 minutes, it is possible for everyone to have given their views and you have a summary of the key issues that can be used to structure other group activities
- **Venn diagrams** can be used for a similar purpose, helping participants identify key issues, and overlaps or connections between them
- There are a variety of ways to get participants to **list** ideas or information, for example, via responses to requests for information on social media platforms or online discussion boards, or in group work by creating 'stations' around the room where participants can list information or ideas on a particular topic. Stations may, for example, be based around themes that emerged from a brainstorm or metaplan (above). These groups may be facilitated or all participants may simply approach each station and contribute individually in their own time
- In the **carousel** technique, participants are assigned to groups (with the same number of groups as there are stations) and given a fixed time to contribute to one station before being rotated to the next. If each group is given its own coloured pen, it is possible for participants to see which ideas were contributed by previous groups. When a group reaches a new station, they are given time to read the contributions of the previous group(s) or these are briefly

summarised by the station's facilitator. They can then query or build upon previous work, listing their own ideas beneath the ideas expressed by previous groups. As the activity continues, it becomes increasingly difficult for groups to add new points, so the time per station can be decreased. Finally, to reduce the time that might otherwise be taken for stations to 'report back' to the wider group, participants can be directed back to their original station, to read what other groups have added to their points. Although not fully comprehensive, this gives everyone a good idea of what has been contributed to all stations. For those who want a fuller picture, the materials can be left on the walls to be viewed during subsequent breaks

Analysing techniques that enable stakeholders to critically evaluate ideas with you include, for example:

- **Categorisation** techniques where participants are asked to sort or group ideas into themes, based on pre-set criteria or based on similarity, for example, the grouping stage of a metaplan, or putting ideas on cards and asking participants to sort the cards into different piles on the basis of their categorisation
- **Mind-mapping**® techniques (also known as concept mapping, spray diagrams, and spider diagrams) can be a useful way to quickly capture and link ideas with stakeholders
- **Problem tree analysis** (also known as cause-effect mapping) is similar to mind-mapping, but is a simpler tool (that is also more limited in the way it can be used). It may be useful in settings where the complexity of a mind-map may be considered intimidating for some participants, or where you purposefully want to keep the analysis simple and brief. Rather than looking at how all issues are linked to one another, problem tree analysis uses the metaphor of a tree to help visualise links between the root causes and solutions to a problem. A simple picture of a tree is drawn on a large piece of paper, with the problem written on the tree trunk. Participants are then asked to draw roots, writing the root causes of the problem along each root. Some root causes may lead to other root causes, so an element of linking may be done between roots, but this should not get too complex. All these roots lead to the bottom of the tree trunk and at the top of the trunk, branches are drawn, along which potential

solutions are written (again with the potential to link branches to other branches to show how one solution may be dependant upon another solution being first implemented). If you want, you can cut out circles of coloured paper to signify fruit, which can be used to represent anticipated impacts or outcomes of implementing solutions

- **SWOT analysis** encourages people to think systematically about the strengths, weaknesses, opportunities and threats as they pertain to the issues being researched
- For issues that have a strong temporal dimension or for project planning with stakeholders, **timelines** can be used to help structure discussion in relation to historical or planned/hoped for future events. There are various ways to do this, for example, flip-chart paper may be placed end-to-end along a wall with a horizontal line along the middle of the paper, marking 'NOW' and specific years and/or historic or known future events, to help people orientate themselves along the timeline. Participants may then write comments or stick post-it notes at various points in the past or future, vertically stacking ideas that occur at the same time

Closing down and deciding techniques include:

- **Prioritisation** differs from ranking by enabling participants to express the strength of their feeling towards a particular option rather than simply saying "yes" or "no" (as in voting) or ranking an idea as better or worse than another idea. Prioritisation exercises also enable you to identify options that are considered to be particularly popular (or not) by participants, which you may then want to explore in greater detail. In prioritisation exercises, participants are given some form of counter that they can assign to different options (e.g. sticky dots or, if working outside, stones, but if you don't have anything to hand, people can simply be asked to assign crosses with pens to options). Normally, participants would each be given a fixed number of counters (at a minimum this should be the same number as the number of options) — this prevents certain participants assigning more counters than other participants to the options they prefer, biasing the outcome. If using sticky dots, it is possible to get people to assign different coloured dots to express their preferences according to different criteria (e.g. use red dots to say how cost-effective they think an idea would be and green dots to express how easily they think the idea would work). It is then

133

possible to see at a glance which ideas are preferred, and it is relatively quick and easy to total the number of counters assigned to all options, and if desired, create a ranked list

- **Multi-Criteria Evaluation** (also known as Multi-Criteria Analysis or Multi-Criteria Decision Modelling) is a decision-support tool for exploring issues and making decisions that involve multiple dimensions or criteria. It allows economic, social and environmental criteria, including competing priorities, to be systematically evaluated by groups of people. Both quantitative and qualitative data can be incorporated to understand the relative value placed on different dimensions of decision options. Broadly, the process involves context or problem definition, representation of evaluation criteria and management options, and evaluation. When applied in a participatory manner with stakeholders, this may involve any of a number of discrete stages, for example:
  - Establishing context and identifying participants: stakeholder mapping/analysis techniques may be used to systematically consider which stakeholders should be involved in the multi-criteria evaluation
  - Defining criteria: criteria are defined that capture stakeholders' interests via facilitated discussion and literature
  - Defining the options that the group is choosing between
  - Scoring options against criteria: the likely performance of each option is scored against each criterion
  - Multi-criteria evaluation: algorithms are used to combine scores and ranks into a weighted value that describes the overall preference towards each option. This may be done either using free software or by hand, adding up scores assigned to each option, and then multiplying scores by agreed amounts for certain criteria (e.g. by 1.5 or 2 depending on whether they are considered to be slightly or much more important than other criteria) and recalculating the scores for each option
  - Discussing the results: this is a decision-support tool so outcomes may be deliberated with participants or amongst decision-makers to assess the degree of consensus, negotiate compromise and manage trade-offs

I've focused on prioritisation methods in this last section because alternatives like voting and ranking can be problematic in my experience. In most group settings, it can be difficult to ensure anonymity in voting, which may bias results, and there is little room to explore reasons for people's voting preferences. Alternatively, ideas can be ranked. However, getting consensus amongst participants for a particular ranking can be challenging, although the discussions that this stimulates may be revealing. It is also not possible to differentiate between options that are particularly popular or unpopular — this may be important if only one or a few ideas are considered viable, as a ranking may imply that mid-ranked options are viable or somewhat preferred.

At the end of your event, you will be left with a mountain of flip-chart paper and post-it notes. It is always a good idea to photograph everything before you remove it from the walls, in case they get lost or damaged in transit back to your office. I often put sticky tape across flip-chart paper that people have stuck post-it notes to, to avoid finding a pile of post-it notes at the bottom of your bag, disconnected from the paper they had been linked to. Be careful to label your folded bits of flip-chart paper so you know which session in your workshop they came from, so it is easier to write up later. Deciphering handwriting and typing this all up yourself can be very time-consuming, so I usually try and get my virtual assistant to do this for me (see Chapter 10). It is important to try and get a report sent to participants as soon as possible after the workshop, even if you don't have time to write much around the tables and photographs that capture the outcomes of the workshop. Make sure you send an accompanying note to anyone who has committed to an action at the end of your workshop. If you don't do this, then there is a danger that people will feel like they have been at a 'talking shop' and it may become hard to re-engage with these people in future work.

Chapter 15
How to facilitate events with stakeholders and members of the public

An experienced professional facilitator is worth their weight in gold. You could run the same event with the same participants, using different facilitators, and get significantly different outcomes. Many researchers think that because they can chair a meeting with other researchers, they can facilitate workshops with stakeholders. This is rarely the case. You will very often be working with very diverse groups with different perceptions of your research, different levels of education and potentially conflicting views. Trying to run a workshop with stakeholders in the same way you would chair a meeting with researchers will rarely get the best out of everyone. In the worst-case scenario, you may end up inflaming conflict and creating long-term difficulties for those you want to work with.

One of the first stakeholder workshops I was charged with designing went horribly wrong when I got the facilitation wrong. It was the first workshop in a funded project that was meant to scope out the potential to conduct a wider research project. The first mistake I made was to ask for the facilitator's day rate when I put the proposal together. When I called her up to engage her for the work, she explained that a one-day workshop involved at least three days of preparation and post-workshop work, so I couldn't afford her. One of my colleagues came to the rescue, recommending an American colleague of his who regularly facilitated stakeholder workshops. For the price of a ticket to a conference, he was happy to facilitate the workshop.

Two things went wrong at the very start. First, our American colleague decided to do a practice run of his conference talk to open the workshop. This might have worked if his talk had something to do with the topic of the workshop, but I could see people shifting uneasily in their seats, wondering if they were at the wrong event. The other thing that was wrong, was that there were three additional people in the room, who I hadn't invited, and I made the mistake of not asking anything about them. Eventually, the workshop started, and people started wheeling out all the old arguments that they'd had for years. The facilitator then stood and watched, saying nothing, as people started raising voices and being rude to each other. The break-time came and went, and still the argument intensified, with the facilitator looking on with a thoughtful expression on his face. At that point, I decided that despite just being a PhD student with no experience of facilitation, this had to stop. So I called time on the arguing and we went to the break. I asked the facilitator why he wasn't facilitating, and he explained that he was American, and everyone was speaking in thick Yorkshire accents, and he couldn't understand a word anyone was saying! So after the break, we moved to a part of the workshop that involved writing things on post-it notes and sticking them on the wall. However, there was a problem. The three people I hadn't invited weren't doing the exercise. I went and explained it to them, and still they didn't do anything. By now, everyone else had completed the task, apart from these three, and all eyes were on me as I explained the task one last time and asked if they understood. They said that they understood. So I asked why they weren't doing it. To my shame, they explained that they were illiterate. I wanted to ground to swallow me up at that moment. I realised that I had humiliated them in front of the very people they wanted to influence in this debate, and I felt horrendous. I announced that we would take an early lunch-break, and asked my facilitator if he had any techniques we could use that didn't involve speaking, reading or writing, to which of course, the answer was, "no". Clearly, this wasn't entirely the fault of the facilitator — I had set him up to fail. But it does illustrate how badly awry things can go when the facilitation goes wrong.

Facilitating dialogue with stakeholders and likely users of research

There are a number of reasons why hiring a professional facilitator (or getting a few facilitation skills of your own) can be particularly useful when engaging with stakeholders and likely users of your research during events, for example:
  • Efficiency: more can be discussed in less time
  • Impartiality
  • Clarity
  • A helpful atmosphere
  • Appropriate techniques
  • More people have a say

- No organisation or individual is in control or has the power of veto
- The outcome is open and more likely to be considered fair by all those involved

Professional facilitation can be expensive, ranging from around £700 to £3000 for a small event, and up to £8000 for a full-day event with over 100 participants. Prices vary with the expertise/reputation of the facilitator and the amount of time necessary to prepare for the event. Unless their role is little more than that of a chairperson to help you steer your way through a simple agenda on time, you are likely to need a number of days of time discussing your aims and coming up with draft facilitation plans that use different techniques to reach these aims. If you want the facilitator to be responsible for writing up the outputs from your event, then this will cost more. It is therefore advisable to build facilitation costs into your research proposal from the outset.

In many projects, there are not sufficient funds to hire a professional facilitator, so we may end up in this role as researchers. When faced with facilitating an event, most of us are understandably nervous.

Some challenges will emerge from the group itself:
- Dominating people with big egos can be hard to manage. You need to learn techniques for keeping these people in check without upsetting them, so that others have a chance to have their say, and feel able to express themselves freely
- Equally, quiet or unconfident people can be hard to manage. You need to find ways of enabling them to contribute to the group without putting people on the spot or intimidating them
- Diverse groups are particularly hard to manage. Groups may be diverse in many different ways, including a mix of quiet and dominant individuals, those with greater or lesser formal educational attainment, those with different levels of power and influence, varying levels of interest in the subject (who are more or less informed about it), and people in a group with very different fundamental values and beliefs

In addition to this, most of us face a number of internal challenges to becoming an effective facilitator. First, we may lack confidence in ourselves. This may be borne of a lack of experience facilitating events with stakeholders, or it may be a deeper-held lack of confidence that we find emerges in all sorts of public situations where we feel others are judging our performance. Whatever the source of this lack of confidence, there are a number of things that can help reduce your nerves, for example:

- Getting practice: although it may not be possible to practise working with stakeholders, there may be other contexts in which we can try out our facilitation tools and skills, for example, by adapting our teaching with students to incorporate tools and skills we know we'll need to use with stakeholders
- Building in buffer time to your facilitation plan (e.g. sessions you can drop or breaks you can shorten), so you're not creating unrealistic expectations from your event, can help reduce nerves on the day
- Have a facilitation team you can trust to come to your rescue if things seem to be going wrong
- Get to the venue early so you can sort out any practical issues in good time before participants arrive
- Get feedback from colleagues on your facilitation plan to make sure it is realistic
- Meet your facilitation team the day before or in good time before your event to go through the facilitation plan and make sure everyone knows what they are doing
- If you know that a certain individual is particularly problematic (e.g. argumentative, confrontational), you may consider having a one-to-one meeting with them separately, rather than inviting them to the event
- Having a Plan B for high-risk activities you have not tried out before can also help reduce your nerves both before and during an event — if a technique isn't working, you know you can change tack. There are also a number of practical tips you can use to keep control of dominating individuals and get the most out of more reticent members of the group (see below)

With practice, there are a number of interpersonal and practical skills that can help you become an effective facilitator. Many of the practical skills are quick and easy to learn, and can make a considerable difference to your practice. However, many of the interpersonal skills are harder to gain. Although some would argue that some of these characteristics are innate and therefore not possible to develop, it may be possible to make efforts to cultivate these characteristics as part of your role as facilitator, though this will take significant time and practice.

It is worth mentioning that interpersonal communication skills are often very culturally specific (though some non-verbal communication transcends cultural differences), so, if you have people from different countries attending, it might be good to know the cultural nuances of those cultures before you go into the room. For example, one of my PhD students, Steven Vella, told me how he once had to jump onto a table and whistle to get the attention of angry stakeholders during a workshop in Malta, threatening to throw everyone out unless they became quiet and asking a member of the project team to apologise for calling them "ignorant locals". This was appropriate in that particular setting, but would have been inappropriate in a UK town hall.

Such interpersonal characteristics of an effective facilitator include, for example, being:
- Perceived as impartial, open to multiple perspectives and approachable
- Capable of building rapport with the group and maintaining positive group dynamics
- Able to handle dominating or offensive individuals
- Able to encourage participants to question assumptions and re-evaluate entrenched positions
- Able to get the most out of reticent individuals
- Humble and open to feedback

Practical facilitation skills include, for example:
- Active listening and understanding. This may include non-verbal feedback such as eye contact, nodding, smiling, focused attention and valuing silence
- Verbal feedback such as sounds, short phrases, clarifying details, encouraging/probing (asking for more information) and using open (not closed) questions
- Giving people time to clarify their thoughts

- Summarising: to confirm that you are interpreting them correctly
- Letting people know their opinions are valued, but without implying that you agree or disagree with them
- Helping people go beyond facts to meanings
- Helping people to 'own' their problems, take responsibility for them and think of solutions
- Reframing points where necessary to help people move from a negative stance to discuss a positive way forward. This involves acknowledging what has been said, and then saying this in a different way that is less confrontational or negative, followed by an open question that seeks to get at the heart of the problem
- Involving others in the group in solving the problem
- Giving momentum and energy
- Ensuring everyone has an opportunity for input without feeling intimidated
- Making an impartial record of the discussion
- Writing clearly, managing paper (ideally with the help of an assistant so you can focus on group dynamics)

Ultimately, to be able to manage power dynamics in a group, facilitators need to have a deep source of their own power. It takes confidence to deal with powerful individuals who are being disrespectful to others in the group. But I'm not just talking about confidence here. It is that thing that you notice in some people, that you can't really put into words; a quiet presence that demands your attention. We have all been in situations where someone walks into the room and you realise that the atmosphere has changed; the conversation might die down and you notice that everyone is waiting for that one person to speak. It is this quiet power that enables the best facilitators to get the most out of the most challenging groups. I would argue that this sort of 'presence' isn't something you are born with, but is something that can be cultivated with commitment and practice.

In Box 12 you'll find a series of questions I've adapted over the years, which are designed to help you understand how powerful you are as an individual in any given context. The answers you give will differ, depending on the context in which you ask the questions, so think specifically of a context in which you would like to have more 'presence', so that you can achieve greater impact, and answer these questions specifically in relation to that context. For example, you might ask how powerful you are in the context of your research team

142

or a group of stakeholders (such as healthcare professionals or conservationists) that you need to be able to work with intensively to achieve impact. The first types of power (hierarchical and social) are fairly hard to do anything about, though promotion might come along once in a while. When doing research in Africa, I found that my race and gender were barriers to working with stakeholders in certain contexts. Simply being aware of the power or powerlessness you are likely to feel in certain contexts may help you avoid trying to facilitate in those situations. However, you can work on your personal and transpersonal power. It takes time and commitment to change these ways of being into habits and eventually into characteristics, but it is possible. When I was Director of the Aberdeen Centre for Environmental Sustainability, I knew that I wasn't the most powerful person in the organisation. It was a PhD student. Since I had joined the organisation, I noticed that whenever she had an idea, people followed, and things happened. Despite being at the bottom of the hierarchy, what she had that I lacked, was bucketloads of personal and transpersonal power. Her life's goal was to make the world a better place and she had enthusiasm and positivity that was infectious and an altruistic vision that inspired hope. Ana ended up working with me as a Post-Doctoral Research Assistant and together we launched the training programme that this book is based on.

Once you've considered the points in Box 12, it can be useful to share your scores with someone you know well. Discuss which categories you score highest in (e.g. most 4 and 5 scores). Where you have low power, can you use higher power from a different area to help you in your interactions with others? Where could you increase your power? Would the person you're discussing this with have scored you differently? If so, why?

Box 12: Identify your levels of power

The following points are designed to help you identify the different types of power you possess in any given context. You can use this in a general sense (thinking about the main social group you belong to or interact with most), but it is most useful to think about how powerful you are in a specific context, for example, as a facilitator leading a workshop with people who are interested in your research. Imagine yourself in this situation, and rate how powerful you feel on a scale of 1–5 in relation to each of the following personal characteristics. You may do this in relation to how powerful you feel and/or how powerful you think the other people in this situation think you are (you will need to chose which of these you think most affects your ability to achieve impact).

Hierarchical power:
- Seniority in formal hierarchy
- Expertise
- Access to decision-makers

Social power:
- Race or ethnicity
- Age
- Gender
- Class or wealth
- Education level
- Strength and breadth of your social networks
- Title (e.g. Mrs, Dr or Prof)

Personal power:
- Self-awareness
- Self-confidence and assertiveness (not over-confidence)
- Charisma and strength of character
- Ability to empathise with others
- Life experience and ability to survive adversity
- Ability to communicate and influence others
- Reputation for integrity and honesty
- Creativity
- Honest estimation of your own worth and abilities, being aware of your limitations and weaknesses, whilst focusing on your strengths and abilities
- Someone who believes in, trusts and builds others up, rather than criticising and gossiping

Transpersonal power:
- Connection to the other; to something larger, more significant and lasting
- Commitment to a positive and clear set of values and beliefs
- Being prepared to challenge the status quo rather than compromise your values
- Ability to overcome or forgive past hurts
- Freedom from fear
- Service to an altruistic vision or cause

Anticipating conflict

Dealing with difficult individuals and situations can be challenging if you've not got a lot of experience as a facilitator. Despite being a professional facilitator myself with experience facilitating over 50 workshops with stakeholders, I wouldn't consider myself to be particularly experienced. If I've got a workshop that is likely to involve conflict or particularly high stakes, I will always try and pay for a more experienced facilitator. But sometimes conflict erupts when we least expect it.

If you've already got to the point where people are having angry outbursts and verbally abusing each other, the chances are it's too late to avoid conflict — you're already in it. But if you can spot the early warnings signs, it may be possible to avert conflict. In my experience, most conflicts with stakeholders arise from power imbalances within the group, so simply identifying particularly high or low power individuals will alert you to the fact that some form of conflict may be likely.

Here are a few of the signs you can look for, to identify people who are (or are perceived by the group or themselves to be) particularly powerful or powerless:

- In some cultures and organisations, the way people dress denotes hierarchical power e.g. male managers in universities often wear suits. Check whether those in your group wearing suits are displaying other signs of high power that could be challenging to manage
- Who does everyone give eye contact to when they speak, and who never gets eye contact? You've probably had that feeling of being invisible when you're in a meeting where everyone else is more powerful than you (the person taking notes in academic meetings usually gets this feeling on a regular basis). Equally, you probably know how awkward it can feel when people in a group only give eye contact to you, as though there's no one else in the room. If there is someone in the room that the group perceives to be particularly important, you'll notice that at some point during each person's speech (usually at the beginning and the end), they will give that individual eye contact, effectively seeking their approval and hoping to win influence with them
- Is there someone in the group who regularly speaks over others and cuts others off? Is there someone in the group who rarely gets to the end of what they're saying, and is there someone else who is always heard out? These are other signs of power and powerlessness that you might spot
- Do you notice that one person's ideas are rarely picked up by the group, perhaps leading to awkward silence or a change of topic? Do you notice that these same ideas may be suggested later on by someone else and be welcomed and discussed actively?
- Who naturally chooses to sit at the head of the table or near the front, and who avoids sitting at the head of the table and chooses to sit at the back?
- Who has a queue of people waiting to speak to them during the break?
- Do some people display particularly confident or nervous/deferential body language?
- Does one person dominate the discussion, offering their opinion on every discussion point?
- Are some people confident enough to give many people in the group eye contact and do others avoid giving people eye contact or only give you eye contact as the facilitator?

147

- Do some people feel so important that they can check their laptop and phone constantly rather than engaging in discussion with the group?

Any single one of these signs may not mean anything, but if there are a few of these signs pointing to particular individuals, you might start to watch those individuals for signs of conflict, and adapt your facilitation plan to avoid power disparities becoming any more obvious. You have to be careful not to mistake personal traits for signs of power imbalances or conflict (e.g. someone who is naturally shy or prone to colourful outbursts). In some cases, it is possible to resolve this through effective facilitation, for example, politely asking more dominant people to give others space to contribute, or using a device like 'round robin' to give every person in the group a chance to give their opinion (or pass to the next person if they do not feel confident doing this). Usually, the simplest solution if you're not an experienced facilitator is to move into small groups or move away entirely from open group discussion and use a structured elicitation technique, like metaplan, where everyone has the same opportunity to contribute.

Here are a few of the signs to watch out for, that might suggest conflict is imminent:
- Are you noticing people closing their body language (e.g. crossing their legs and arms, dropping eye contact etc.)?
- Are people becoming cold, distant, withdrawn (e.g. moving back from the table, giving one word answers etc.)?
- People often dress up insults as jokes to make it socially acceptable for them to attack someone else and to make it hard for others to criticise them for their comment ("I was only joking"). Look to see who is smiling at the joke — and more importantly who is not smiling. If the person the joke is aimed at is colouring up, the chances are they took the joke as an insult. You might be too late to do anything about it first time round, but you need to watch the situation like a hawk and politely stamp on any future 'jokes', if you want to maintain a positive group dynamic
- Are people becoming increasingly argumentative, disagreeing and/or blaming each other?
- Are people moralising or intellectualising each other?

But for the really early warning signs of conflict, you need to look inside yourself and empathise with the group you're working with. If you can really get in touch with the way that the group is feeling, and become sensitive enough to your own feelings, you will start to detect the earliest glimmer of conflict and be able to watch out for other signs and act early. If there's someone in the room who is feeling really uncomfortable, nervous or angry in the group, the chances are they may project those feelings onto you, or that you may detect their feelings through empathy — and you'll start feeling uncomfortable, nervous or angry yourself. Are you experiencing irrational, unaccountable feelings, urges or thoughts, or acting uncharacteristically out of role? It is likely that this is how someone in the group is feeling. The stronger they feel this, and the more people who feel this way, the more likely you are to pick up on it and experience those feelings yourself. In this way, you can pick up on likely conflict well before there are any visible signs, so you can manage the situation and bring back a more positive dynamic into the group before conflict erupts.

Useful techniques for avoiding conflict

Finally, here are some useful tips you can use to avoid conflict and get the most out of facilitating events with stakeholders:

- Set some ground rules: agree them at the outset, and refer back if needed (people are not to talk over one another, everyone's views should be equally respected, no use of offensive language etc). It may be useful to write these down and place them on the wall for everyone to see. It is typically easy to agree such rules as a group at the outset. They can be particularly useful if someone becomes obstructive or abusive later in the event. If you are unable to keep them in check, you can remind them about the ground rules that the whole group agreed to at the start. Given that they were part of the group that agreed these rules, it is socially quite difficult for them to ignore them, and if they do continue to ignore these rules, you have a clear basis upon which to ask them to leave
- Any Other Business (or 'parking space'): if you have someone who finds it hard to be concise and in particular if contributions are off-topic, it is possible to create a 'parking space' where you can write these ideas up and park them to discuss later. This technique only works if the group has jointly agreed to the aims of the event at the outset, and if you have the flexibility to create a 15–20 minute session at

149

the end to deal with the points that are parked. By parking less relevant ideas for later, you can keep the discussion focused and on time. Experience suggests that by the end of the event, it will have become clear to all participants that the points that were parked were not relevant and hence the person who suggested them tends to opt to ignore them at this point. Where points are deemed worth covering, you have created time to deal with them, which prevents these points eating into the rest of your time. Also, because it is done at the end of the meeting, participants are usually keen to finish the event and have an incentive to be more concise at that point

- Open space: if you discover that your aims do not match the aims of some of your participants, this can be difficult to deal with if you want to keep everyone in the room with you and satisfied with the outcomes. A simple technique is to use some of the buffer time you built into your facilitation plan (e.g. a session you can drop or a break you can curtail) to create an 'open space' discussion. Using this approach, the additional topics that participants want to cover are collected (and grouped if there are many points). Participants then have the option to sign up to topics of particular interest to them over the next break (at this point it will become apparent if some of the topics were just the interest of one vocal proponent, as others don't sign up for that group), and then you facilitate small group discussions, recording points and feeding them back to the wider group. If you don't have enough facilitators to do this, you may ask the person who proposed each topic to facilitate their group

- Empathise with and mirror your group: get a sense of how the group is feeling (e.g. bored, tired or angry) and adapt your approach to their needs. Empathy is about putting yourself in other people's shoes, so you need to connect with their feeling, identifying with it in some way, such as by voicing it or mimicking it via body language (or both). Then you can start to counter feelings that are likely to negatively affect group dynamics, gradually changing your body language, tone of voice and language to become increasingly open, up-beat and interested. Although this can take significant effort, you will be surprised at how many start to mirror and begin feeling and acting in more positive ways

Chapter 16
How to use social media to drive research impact without wasting your time

A lot of researchers waste a lot of time on social media. I'm not talking about sharing funny photos of cats (though many of us find this an enjoyable way to waste time of course). I'm talking about those of us who engage with social media professionally, but without any particular plan or goal. I'm going to suggest in this chapter that if you aren't working with the public and haven't identified any stakeholders in your research who are likely to engage with social media, then there's no point trying to use social media to generate research impact. It won't work.

Of course, there are many other great reasons for engaging with social media professionally: connecting and keeping up with colleagues around the world, for example, during and after conferences; managing to get in touch with inaccessible professors and politicians who don't reply to their emails; being first to hear about funding opportunities and the latest research in your field; the list goes on.

I know many academics who have invested incalculable hours writing a weekly blog that virtually no one reads, or who distract themselves with Twitter throughout the day without actually driving any new interest in their research (or getting much useful information). My hope is that by the end of this chapter, you will find out how you can use social media efficiently, so you don't have to spend much time away from your research, but get significant rewards for the time you do invest, because you invest your time on social media strategically.

Can social media deliver research impact?

You might be surprised how many of us use social media in some shape or form on a regular basis. The reason you might be surprised is that you are probably already using technologies that could be classified as social media without realising it.

There are lots of complex academic definitions of social media, but I think you can boil them all down to:

Public conversations that take place through digital media.

Using this definition means that You Tube is actually a form of social media, because you can reply to a video with a video of your own, and there are often long public conversations about the content of videos in the comments underneath. Blogs are a type of social media (when they work and people comment on them). Wikipedia can be considered a type of social media if you consider the number of people engaging with and editing the content of some entries. Figure 9 lists some of the other platforms that are currently available.

Typically, around 90% of the researchers I train from all career stages use social media in some way on a regular basis. However, the proportion of researchers actively using social media in their research is actually much lower. An estimate in 2008 put the figure at 1 in 40. For the groups I train, the figure is usually between 20 and 30% of participants.

Figure 9: Examples of social media platforms

152

Here are the top reasons cited by researchers I train who already use social media professionally:

1. You can use social media to get feedback on new research ideas, so that you can reframe them to be more relevant to the people who might use your findings
2. You can get insights into the way that likely users of your research are talking about the topics you're working on — the kind of language they are using and the sorts of things they're most interested in. These sorts of insights can be invaluable when you need to start communicating your findings
3. You can be the first to find out about news and events related to your research, and you can link your own work to what's happening, making it more likely that your work is picked up and debated
4. An increasing number of researchers are finding out about funding on social media (particularly Twitter). You can also identify collaborators for grant proposals, who you already trust to be good team players through your online interactions with them. You can find out about funding that you might not have come across through your institution, especially linked to industry, which can help generate impacts from research
5. You can take part in discussions around academic conferences using conference hashtags that are used to aggregate content relating to that particular event. You can stay in touch with academics you meet at conferences and elsewhere more easily, and have the opportunity to interact with leaders in your research field on different continents who you might not otherwise meet or be able to interact with.

What surprises me is how few researchers use social media professionally to drive impact from their work. There are a number of good reasons why many researchers do not use social media professionally, let alone with impact in mind.

Why don't more researchers use social media in their work?

Given all these benefits, why aren't more researchers using social media professionally? There are a number of good reasons for limited engagement:

- Time is the number one reason more researchers aren't using social media at all, or if they are, why they're not using it professionally. Most researchers struggle to read and reply to their emails, let alone have to read and reply to the volume of material available on social media as part of their work day
- A close second is privacy. Researchers don't want to share their personal lives with their colleagues or the wider world, and many worry about their social media accounts being hacked, leading to identity theft and reputational damage
- The other common reason I hear from researchers is: "I've got nothing useful to say, and even if I did, I couldn't say it in 140 characters" (the character limit for tweets)
- Finally, there are genuine concerns that using social media professionally could get people into trouble — ill-chosen words on social media have, after all, cost many people their jobs.

All of these are genuine and real concerns, and it is important to be aware of these issues before you consider whether or not you should be engaging with social media in your work. If you read this chapter and come to the conclusion that the risks are too high, and that you will not use social media in your research, then I will still have done my job. All I want is for researchers to take a serious look at the risks and benefits, and make an informed decision about whether or not to use these tools. What I'd like to avoid is people deciding not to engage out of fear or because they believe some of the greatest myths about social media for researchers.

The four greatest myths about social media for researchers

Most people who do not use social media in their research do so for
good reasons. But I think many of the reasons people give for not
engaging with these technologies are in fact myths. I believe that
these are the four greatest myths about social media for researchers:

1. "Productive researchers don't have time to waste on social media"

Do you read or watch the news most days? If so, then you probably
have a news-shaped space in your daily routine. The problem with
the mass media that most of us consume, however, is that it is not
very targeted. You have to wade through pages of newsprint or listen
to or watch a whole broadcast to catch the few items that really
interest you. I'm not saying that you should stop engaging with print
and broadcast media, but what if you were to cut down the amount of
time you spent on that, and filled that time back up again with highly
specific news that's particularly relevant to you? Wouldn't this time
be better spent? What if, during that news-shaped space in your
schedule, you'd heard about the latest discoveries in your field, found
out about a grant you could apply for and kept abreast of policy
developments or commentary relating to issues you are researching?
Would that be time wasted or would that actually make you more
productive? I have found out about funding opportunities and found
collaborators for grants (that I've subsequently won) through social
media, and that definitely wasn't a waste of time.

What about all that frivolous stuff you hear about on social media all
the time? You don't want to watch any more cat videos. Fair enough.
Me neither. The great thing about most social media platforms is that
you can unfollow or mute the people who are boring you with endless
pictures of their pets. I work on my signal-to-noise ratio all the time,
unfollowing or muting people whose material isn't relevant enough to
be worth my time. The result is a tailored news stream of highly
relevant material whenever I've got time to look at it.

Apparently people are no good at waiting any more — the evidence is
that in any place where people wait, everyone nowadays seems to be
on their smart phone. I don't think I'm particularly bad at waiting, but
I hate wasting time, and having access to social media on my smart
phone means I can learn and be productive, even with small windows
of time that would otherwise have been wasted. What about just
being mindful, I hear you say? Well I'm up for that, but I'd prefer to
schedule some quality time for prayer or meditation and engage with

social media in a mindful way (see the strategic approach that follows).

I have almost 20,000 followers across my social media accounts, and that grows by between 50-100 followers per day. You would think I must spend hours on social media every day, but the reality is surprising. I typically spend about 20 minutes per day on social media, and about 10 minutes on traditional news media. I manage three Twitter accounts and my LinkedIn and Facebook account on a daily basis and engage with other platforms on a more sporadic basis, like Pinterest, Vine, Periscope and Google+. My point is that you don't have to spend all day on social media to become influential in this sphere. Box 13 describes the tips I use to grow my influence online, and I will unpack these in the next chapter.

If you're thinking that's easy for someone at my career stage, but not achievable if you are an early career researcher, then take a look at Rosmarie Katrin Neumann (Twitter handle @RosmarieKatrin). She crowdfunded part of her first year as my PhD student, before she was awarded her scholarship at Newcastle University. Over her first four months on Twitter, she attracted 55 followers. Then she started using the technique in Box 13 and the tips in the following chapter. Within the next three and a half months, she reached 1000 followers (including many of the big names in her field). This is not only important for her visibility as a researcher, but also to build networks as she is starting her own business as a knowledge broker alongside her PhD. She needs her ever-growing network to make people aware of the services she provides. She spends between 15 and 30 minutes per day on Twitter, including catching up on news and following/unfollowing people linked to her interests. Anyone can do this, and it doesn't have to displace other work.

I don't want this to come across as suggesting that our goal should always be to amass as many followers as possible. The focus, if we want to generate impact should be on the quality of engagement you can derive from your use of social media. In many cases, a small but highly engaged and relevant following is far better for achieving this. However, for certain purposes, you may want to become influential on social media, and for that you need to be well known. I have different strategies for different projects. For my peatland (@IUCNpeat) and desertification (@DESIREproject) Twitter accounts, I'm focusing on providing balanced, up-to-date evidence to inform policy and practice. I tweet once a week for one and once a month for the other, and don't have a strategy for growing my followers on those accounts. However, for my knowledge exchange and impact research (@fasttrackimpact), I had given myself a target of reaching 10,000 followers before I launched my free online training course for researchers, because I wanted to have enough influence and visibility to be able to make the course widely available. It was an ambitious goal, given that it had taken me three years to amass 2,500 followers, and I only gave myself three months to reach 10,000.

Box 13: How to get 50–100 new followers per day (and only spend 20 minutes a day on Twitter)

- Have a social media strategy: know your audience, add value to them and actively promote
- Focus on Twitter (and LinkedIn if you've got time)
- Be credible: link to content
- Be visual: stand out from the crowd
- Tweet at the right time: audience time zone and engagement peak times
- Three tweets and a follow/unfollow strategy

For more details about how to do each of these things, see the next chapter.

This is just one strand of a wider social media strategy for that part of my research, which is focused on training as many researchers internationally as possible by 2020, when I hope to have generated enough profits to commission independent research on the effect that this has had on these researchers' impact. Because the training is based on my research, and every new piece of research in this area that I do gets integrated into the course, my hope is to be able to submit the impact of this research for evaluation under the next Research Excellence Framework. My point is that I have a unique social media strategy for this particular thread of my research, which is embedded in a wider impact plan for this work. I'm using social media to achieve specific, measurable impact goals. I'm not able to measure how much of an impact the researchers who do my course are having yet, but I am able to measure whether I reached my 10,000 follower target (I got there 26 days late, but I got there) and whether that translated into researchers signing up for my free course. As I explained in Chapters 3 and 9, it is as important to track the success of your knowledge exchange as it is to track your impacts. How will you know if you are on track to achieve your impacts if you have no idea that your knowledge exchange activities aren't working? The nice thing about social media is that as a form of knowledge exchange, it is very easy to track your progress.

2. "Social media will intrude on my personal life"

Okay, if you've got an addictive personality, this might not be a myth: proceed with caution. But assuming you can manage the temptation to check your social media networks at every opportunity, I think many people's privacy concerns are very real, but entirely manageable.

First, you don't have to put photos of your breakfast on social media — that choice is entirely yours. You don't even have to post things — you can simply use social media to consume material. Second, you can set most social media platforms to only allow those you want to see your content. Even though I don't have many friends on Facebook, and many are family members, I never post personal stuff, and I've got it set so that if others post personal stuff about me, I get to review it first before it appears on my timeline and the timelines of my friends. Third, you can choose to only use social media from your computer and if you do have it on your smart phone, you can choose to turn off the notifications so they don't intrude on your personal life.

3. "No one would be interested in anything I've got to say anyway"

You don't have to say anything. Most people start their use of social media as 'lurkers' — they watch what other people are saying, and use social media purely as a form of news. Many people stay in that mode of engagement, which is still really useful. However, most people then graduate to liking, sharing or retweeting the things they find most useful. If you stop at this point, that's also great. Now you're not only benefiting from what other people are saying; you're adding value to others like you who are following your updates. Many researchers engage with social media in these two modes for years before they post any of their own material. So the point is, you don't have to have anything interesting to say to benefit from engaging professionally with social media.

Finally, it is worth saying that when I give people the challenge of summarising their research area or a recent finding in 140 characters or less, there is very rarely anyone who can't do it, and the things you learn about people's work from what they've written can be fascinating. Being forced to be concise and simple in our language can be difficult for many academics, but it is surprising how engaging you can be when you try. And finally, even if you really can't find anything particularly interesting to say about your research, there is a very high probability that other researchers in your field will find it very interesting. Although that may not drive impact, it can still help you build your professional networks.

4. "Social media will get me into trouble"

One academic told me that he had banned himself from social media because he couldn't trust himself not to say something he'd regret after a couple of glasses of wine on a Friday night. For most of us though, the chances of something going badly wrong are fairly remote if you exercise a bit of sensible caution. We've all heard about high-profile people losing their jobs over misjudged tweets, but part of the reason that they lose their jobs and we hear about it is because of their profile. You just have to look at the horrendous things that trolls say without consequence to realise that there is a lot of latitude in what people can get away with. However, as researchers, we don't want to be just getting away with it — we have our professional reputation to protect. So, my advice is to be super careful online and remember that everything you say is on the public record. You can say far more on a public stage than you can on social media, because of the way comments online can be taken out of context so easily.

For example, I once got into a debate with someone on Twitter and said something mildly disrespectful about a Guardian journalist who had been criticising my research. Of course, the journalist was following the conversation, and wasn't happy about what I said. Although I thought the comment was justifiable, I knew that the tone was wrong, and I instantly apologised, publicly in a tweet. The others who were following the conversation were disappointed that I'd called time on the debate just as it was getting interesting, and it turned out that the organiser of the Hay Festival was one of them, and we were both invited to publicly debate the issue on stage. Luckily for me, it never happened (I'm sure I'd have been eaten for breakfast). But the strange thing is that I would have felt comfortable saying what I said on Twitter and much more face-to-face in a live debate. On another occasion, I arrived late to speak at an event in Windsor Castle (after getting it mixed up with the Tower of London — oops) and missed the bit where they said it was Chatham House Rules (where you're not allowed to reveal the identity of those present), and got into trouble for tweeting a photo that showed who was attending the meeting. So yes, social media *can* get you into trouble, but for most of us, with a bit of care, getting into serious trouble is extremely unlikely.

I believe that the opposite is far closer to the truth nowadays: *not having a positive digital footprint* will get me into trouble. Perhaps it is an overstatement to say that abstaining from digital media will "get you into trouble", but in many situations nowadays, it doesn't do you any favours. Of course, a negative digital footprint is far worse than no footprint at all. Google yourself and see if material from your student days still comes up, and get rid of it. But for most academics, the bigger problem is their lack of digital footprint, beyond the page on their institution's website, which is usually woefully out of date.

When I'm hiring a new post-doc or evaluating candidates for academic posts, I always Google them, and I know many others who do the same. If I can't find a digital footprint, then I start to ask questions. Is this person really doing internationally leading research if I can't find it easily on the Internet? Do they have something to hide? If nothing else, make sure you've got a Google Scholar profile and a ResearchGate profile (Figure 10).

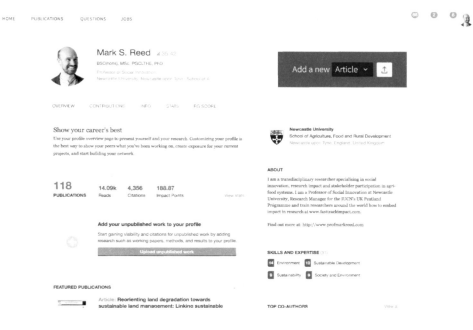

Figure 10: Google Scholar and ResearchGate profiles

How to use social media to drive research impact without wasting time

When I was asked to apply for my current Chair position, I tried to protest that I was in the middle of my longest ever losing streak for research funding and that I could never live up to the reputation of the retiree who had vacated the Chair (who is my all-time academic hero). I was told that my record spoke for itself, according to my website, and that I should think about it. The majority of plenary talks I'm invited to give come via my website, and I've built an international training business through social media, without ever once paying for advertising. Time invested building and curating your digital footprint really can pay dividends for your career.

More important than all this, having a strong digital brand as an academic engenders credibility and trust among many of the people who you might like to use your research, making it easier for you to connect with them. The next section shows you how you can harness the power of social media to drive research impact. If you use social media strategically, as I'm going to suggest, then it doesn't have to take up huge amounts of time. It doesn't have to intrude on your personal life or get you into trouble. And you may discover, to your surprise, that you've actually got some quite interesting things to say, that other people find both engaging and useful.

Researchers are in a unique position on social media, because we have easily verifiable credibility as authoritative voices. Box 14 uses a fascinating (though somewhat grisly) example to illustrate how this works. Although it is unlikely that any research finding would ever 'go viral' to the extent that the information in Box 14 did, it is possible for researchers to achieve significant reach via social media. I once did an experiment with a government department to see if we could use Twitter to get public feedback on a policy consultation. The experiment failed because (as you could probably have told me), no one was able to provide meaningful feedback in 140 characters. However, it did raise awareness of the consultation, with some of our tweets reaching a potential audience of over 40,000 people.

Figure 11: Screenshots of Twitter analytics for one month from Twitter.com

An analysis of @fasttrackimpact over a month on Twitter shows that my 41 tweets that month were seen by 337,000 people on Twitter (Twitter's definition of "impressions") (Figure 11). 124 people mentioned me in their tweets, 18,000 people viewed my Twitter profile to find out more about Fast Track Impact, and I got 2,421 new followers that month (a 90 day average of 82 new followers per day). Twitter's analytics even tell me the interests of my followers and demographic information that might help me further tailor my messages to my audience. These statistics may not be "viral", but they illustrates the power of social media to disseminate messages. Karine Nahon and Jeff Hemsley, in their book *Going Viral*, suggest that:

"…a viral information event creates a temporally bound, self-organised interest network in which membership is based on an interest in the information content or in belonging to the interest network of others."

Believe it or not, as researchers, we can create a "viral information event" based on our research. In fact, as researchers, we have an advantage over almost anyone else if we want to be listened to. Research from the 1950s showed that people are more likely to adopt the position of a source if they perceive that source to be credible.

People are surprisingly discerning in what they trust and believe on social media, and if you have a link to your institutional webpage and are clearly who you say you are, you have instant credibility in the eyes of many social media users. This means that our voices carry weight in this sphere, and this gives us an immediate head start if we want to communicate our research to a wide audience and engage people in conversations about our work online. Although we might constantly tell our students to check their sources and use peer-reviewed material, the average person, including many decision-makers, rely on anecdotal evidence that they find online. Instead of worrying about this, we can do something about it by adding our voice to the debate and making high-quality evidence accessible to those who are debating the issues we research. To do this, however, we need to go beyond digital dissemination and online marketing to having digital conversations.

Most academics use social media without any clear plan — they're just putting out material and hoping for the best. But if you really want to harness the power of social media to generate impact from your research, you need a plan. If you don't have a plan, then you may well be blogging and tweeting into empty space. It doesn't take long to think strategically about your use of social media, but when you do, you'll discover that your time on social media has never been better spent. With a clear plan of who you're trying to reach and why, you can take your use of social media to a completely new level.

Seven questions to take your use of social media to a new level

All you have to do is answer seven questions, and you'll have your very own social media strategy. You don't have to write it down, but if you do want to formalise it a bit more, you can use the template in Part 4 of this book. Keep the answers to these questions in mind before you tweet, blog or do anything else, and you'll make every minute you spend on social media count towards making an impact.

1. What do you want to achieve through social media?

Come up with a few SMART objectives (specific, measurable, attainable, relevant, and time-bound) and think about how these objectives might support your organisation's mission, and crucially therefore how your organisation can support you in achieving your goals on social media.

2. Who are you trying to reach through social media and what are they interested in?

Start by asking yourself who is likely to be interested in your research and who might use it? What aspects of your research are they most likely to be interested in, and how might they use your findings? Think of as many different groups or types of people and organisations as you can, and consider whether they will be interested in different aspects of your work. Use this to come up with a few different key messages from your work that these different audiences might be interested in.

Box 14: The role of credibility in viral communication

At 21.45 Eastern Time on 1 May 2011, the US White House announced that President Obama would be addressing the nation in 45 minutes time. Naturally, rumours rapidly began to circulate, attempting to guess what the announcement would be about. Two theories began to circulate, that either Muammar Gaddafi, former ruler of Libya, or Osama Bin Laden had been caught. However, neither theory gained particular traction until the appearance of the now famous tweet by Keith Urbahn, chief of staff to Donald Rumsfeld, 38 minutes after the news conference was officially announced. It was his position, visible on his Twitter profile that gave him the credibility to overcome the rumours and initiate one of the best-documented viral events on social media.

Despite only having 1000 followers on Twitter, after one minute, there had been 80 reactions (retweets and mentions), and this reached 300 after 2 minutes. In that second minute, New York Times reporter, Brian Stelter tweeted, "*Chief of staff former defense sec. Rumsfeld, @keithurbahn, tweets: 'I'm told by a reputable person they have killed Osama Bin Laden.*"

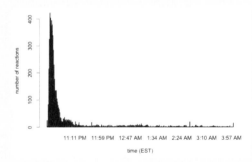

Number of times Keith Urbahn's tweet was retweeted

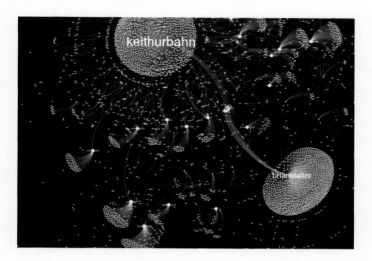

Brian Stelter had 50,000 followers, and his tweet was retweeted hundreds of times in a matter of minutes. Twenty-four minutes after Keith Urbahn's original tweet, the news was being mentioned on Twitter 30,000 times per minute. What is particularly interesting about this example is that many others were guessing correctly before Keith Urbahn's tweet, and rumours about Colonel Gaddafi continued to circulate without ever taking off. The key reason that this tweet initiated a viral information event, was the credibility of the source.

As a researcher, if you link to your institutional webpage and/or mention your university in your Twitter profile, you instantly have credibility in the eyes of the average Twitter user (whether you deserve it or not). This means that your voice can carry weight in discussions on social media.

Images from socialflow.com

167

3. How can you easily find relevant content?

To make life easier and keep a steady flow of material on your key messages, have a look at what you and your colleagues are already doing with traditional and other forms of digital media. Identify content that can be repurposed, remixed, or recycled for your social media strategy. Did you just integrate your findings into a conference talk or lecture? Can you put the slides online (e.g. via SlideShare)? Can you turn your speech notes or the class handout into a blog? Can you repurpose material for use on multiple networks, for example, posting longer versions of key tweets as Facebook and LinkedIn posts? Bear in mind that there are different styles, conventions and types of content suited to different networks. Something with a slightly more personal edge might work well on Facebook, but everything needs to be strictly professional on LinkedIn. Pinterest and Instagram will need a powerful image (and this is also a major bonus for the Google+ interface).

4. Who can you work with to make your use of social media more efficient and effective?

Malcolm Gladwell, in his book *The Tipping Point*, suggests that any "idea epidemic" depends on a small number of individuals with specific skills: mavens, connectors and salespeople. Most academics are 'mavens' — ideas people. This is handy for generating new content, but the problem is that far fewer academics are effective 'salespeople'. You may have the ideas, but you may not have the words that will get your ideas to resonate with a wide audience. But there may be someone in your team or your social network who has that knack, and if they do, then you need to try and tap into that. Send them your findings and ask them to tweet it or blog about it for you, and then learn from and paraphrase the messages that gain most traction in your own messaging.

There is one other type of person who can be very handy to have in your team or network if you want to get your messages out far and wide — especially if you want to get your messages out to quite diverse audiences that wouldn't normally interact with each other much. 'Connectors' are those people you know who always know someone who can help, and if they don't know directly they'll know someone you can ask. They often 'bridge' disparate social networks with contacts and followers from many different walks of life. In the world of social media these people often have large followings and can be influential in getting your messages heard. Start by getting to know them a bit — follow their work and interact with them if you can. Then ask them directly if they would disseminate or repost your material (e.g. retweet, like, blog about or give you a guest blog). If they don't respond via social media, find an email address for them, and if that doesn't work, pick up the phone. Although people are sometimes a bit surprised, I've never had anyone refuse when I've done this (as an aside, I just hired a communications manager who it turns out I called years ago to retweet something because her Twitter feed was so influential — it's a small, connected world). So find the mavens, connectors and salespeople in your team and network (and those who are all three) and work out how you can work together more effectively.

5. How can you make your content actionable, shareable and rewarding for those who interact with you?

What do you want to get people who engage with your social media messages to do? What do you want them to share and what might make it attractive for them to share this? What will they gain personally from doing what you're asking them to do and sharing your message?

6. How can you monitor and evaluate your social media plan? Identify metrics you can use to assess whether you are being successful or not. Consider whether you want to measure this entirely in terms of interaction or if you can look at ways in which your engagement with social media is leading to measurable impacts on society. How will you use this data to improve your practice? Is there a small element of your plan that you can pilot with a particular audience? How will you collect and implement feedback?

7. How does your social media strategy contribute towards your wider impact strategy?

Not all impacts will arise through social media — in fact most are probably going to arise from face-to-face interactions (which of course may come about via social media connections). Not all of the audiences that will be interested in your research will be on social media. To see how these strategies fit together, take a look at the example impact plan for a research project in Part 4, which includes social media as one of many pathways to impact.

I'll conclude this chapter with an example of a social media campaign I helped with, linked to my research. We drew on marketing literature, which suggests that the most successful social media campaigns contain elements of "do, share and gain". Led by Project Maya (www.mayaproject.org), the Sustainable Uplands project helped develop a #peatfree campaign in September 2014 to promote the use of peat-free composts instead of peat-based composts, which are leading to the destruction of lowland peat bog habitats around the world.

Box 15: Example of a social media campaign by researchers

In September 2014, Project Maya launched a campaign to get gardeners to pledge to use peat-free compost (the #peatfree pledge) in order to raise awareness of the value of our peatlands and put a halt to the use of peat for compost. The campaign included infographics and linked these to a website and information on the research behind the campaign and a link to enable gardeners to pledge to use peat-free compost. 'Peat Compost' was chosen as many people used the product. The knowledge that using this product caused destruction to peatlands was unexpected, and the infographics illustrated this impact visually, using unexpected facts aimed to shock, making it visceral.

Box 16: Make it PUVV

Successful online engagement is:
- **Personal**: Create designs with a personal hook in mind and ensure the campaign cultivates the feeling of personal relevance.
- **Unexpected**: People like consuming and then sharing *new* information. Work to pique their curiosity and reframe the familiar.
- **Visual**: It is important to show, don't tell! Use photos and visuals.
- **Visceral**: A campaign that triggers the senses and taps into emotions is much more likely to be successfully shared.

To 'share something' they created a "peat-free pledge" for people to sign and then share via various social media platforms to show their commitment to buying peat-free composts in future (Box 15). Marketing literature also suggests that people engage with content that personally affects them, that is visual, novel and/or connects with them emotionally. Therefore, the most successful online engagement keeps the PUVV principles in mind: personal, unexpected, visual and visceral (Box 16). The campaign caught the attention of the Horticultural Growers Association, who invited me to discuss the issue with them, and I was invited by government to become one of only two non-industry members of a task force to phase out the use of peat composts in the UK.

Chapter 17
How to get impact from Twitter, You Tube and LinkedIn

How can Twitter enhance the impact of your research?

Twitter is one of the most powerful social media platforms for academics, given the number of highly focused and influential networks of people who use it. Effective use of Twitter doesn't just amplify your research, it enables conversations to take place about it. This can enrich your research and enable you to make a far greater impact.

1. Tweet yourself, your projects and your institution

In addition to your personal Twitter profile, consider opening accounts for some of your research groups or projects. Each of your research projects is likely to have a different focus, and you're probably a member of more than one group or institution in your university that doesn't have a Twitter account. A project Twitter account is an easy addition to your next Pathways to Impact statement when you're applying for funding, and some sort of engagement with social media is increasingly expected by reviewers.

Opening an institutional account will usually need to be a group decision. If everyone agrees, others can either send you material to tweet or you can give everyone the Twitter username and password to tweet themselves (if so, you'll need to agree on the nature of material you want posted, or it may be easier to decide on the things you want to avoid).

Open accounts for major research projects that will be going for a few years, and that you hope will have some form of successor project in the future (so you've got time to build a following and don't have too many accounts to manage). Again, the burden doesn't have to be entirely yours — it can be delegated to a post-doc and shared with other team members. Other ideas you might want to consider:

1. Link to your Twitter feed from your project/institution homepage, and include the link in newsletters, presentations and consider putting it in your email signature
2. Every time you do a conference/workshop/seminar presentation, put your slides online (e.g. using SlideShare) and tweet them
3. Every time you get a paper published, tweet the link to the article on the publisher's website (if it's not open access, consider adding that you can send copies if need be). If you can get permission, upload a copy on ResearchGate or similar and tweet the link
4. Tweet quotes from speakers at conferences you attend, using the conference hashtag (make one up if there isn't one), to connect with other delegates and make them aware of your work
5. Set up Science Direct (or something similar) and Google News and Google Scholar alerts for key words and authors that are particularly relevant to your work, so you can be the first to let your followers know about new developments linked to your shared interests
6. When you've got a tweet that's of much wider, general interest, you can retweet it from your other project/institutional accounts, to reach a much larger audience than you could ever command from your personal account or one project
7. Next time you're revising your website, why not consider adding buttons to enable readers to share what they're reading via Twitter and other social media platforms?

2. Don't just wait for people to find you: actively promote your Twitter stream

There are some easy things you can do to promote your Twitter stream, like including links on your homepage, project websites and in your email signature. But more active promotion of your Twitter feed can attract many more followers:

- Make sure you've got an effective biography (consider including some popular and relevant hashtags in it if possible) and enough really informative/useful (typically with a link to more information) tweets in your stream before actively marketing what you're doing

- Contact relevant people with large followings to ask if they would retweet key messages you've sent — tweet or direct message them via Twitter, and if that doesn't work, find their email address via an internet search and email (or phone) them
- Use hashtags (#) to make your tweets visible to more people (e.g. #PhDchat) — notice which hashtags people you're following are using, and use them. If you're planning a Twitter campaign on a particular topic (e.g. linked to a new paper or policy brief), you could make up your own hashtag, but for it to work, others will need to use it, so you may want to work on getting a key tweet including your hashtag retweeted by others with larger followings.

The way most people find out about other people on Twitter is when they get followed. Default settings send an email and mobile notification to a user when a new person starts following them (including their brief biography) — if they like what they read, chances are they will follow you. Twitter recommendations (on www.twitter.com) can be helpful, but it will only recommend a few people and recommendations are less relevant when you're just starting out. If you log out of Twitter and search for your profile on the website, Twitter will list others who are similar to you on the basis of who they follow and who follows them, compared to you. But the best way to find others who may be interested in what you're doing is to see who is following other users who are tweeting very similar things to you:

- Who are the people you most frequently retweet? Whose tweets are you most likely to follow links from? Go to these people's profiles and see who is following them, then systematically follow their followers

- If you have time, try and be a bit selective — you can usually filter out the least relevant people from their username (e.g. don't bother following companies that are clearly just following the person to try and get their custom)

- Most people will decide whether or not to follow you based on the last three tweets you wrote, so before you start following lots of people strategically, make sure your last three tweets are representative of the sort of thing you tweet about, and among your best (e.g. look back through your historic tweets to see if there was something you wrote a few weeks or months ago that was popular, which you could tweet again)

- If you're following people who are following a specific Twitter account, make sure that one of your most recent three tweets is either a retweet from the account you're targeting or a quoted retweet with your take on the story, so that followers instantly recognise that you're tweeting about material they're familiar with

- Twitter monitors the ratio of people following you to the number of people you follow to stop spammers, so you will reach a limit beyond which you cannot follow anyone else. But don't let that stop you getting the word out about what you're doing. Unlike on Facebook, it is common and acceptable to unfollow users (they won't be notified that you unfollowed them) to free up room to follow others. If possible, unfollow the people who you've been following for longest who have not followed you back (so you give people as long as possible to notice you've followed them and they have time to check you out). Tools like ManageFlitter, Crowdfire, Unfollow for Twitter, iUnfollow and UnfollowSpy can make strategic unfollowing very quick and easy. Note that each of these websites and apps will only allow you to unfollow a set number of people every day unless you pay. However, if you do pay for unlimited unfollows, Twitter can revoke authorisation from the website or app to your account for unfollowing too many people (and the website or app will no longer work for you), so it is best not to pay for these services.

One problem with this approach is that you'll no longer be able to use this account to follow tweets from the people you're most interested in learning from (as they'll be lost in the noise of all the other tweets from people you just wanted to know you existed). To ensure you can still use Twitter to gather information from those you're most interested in, either make sure you only market your project or institutional Twitter accounts in this way, or set up a 'personal' Twitter account where you follow those you're most interested in and a 'work' Twitter account that follows many more people, where you put out most (if not all) of your tweets. Lists can also be useful for this — set up a list of users who tweet in different areas so you can look at a more selective timeline of tweets that interest you.

3. Work on your signal-to-noise ratio

As an academic, you need to build your reputation in your chosen field. Twitter can help you reach a network of highly relevant academics, as well as potential users of your research, and make them aware of your work. To do this effectively, you need to decide what it is that you want to be 'known' for, and then work on building your reputation in that area. Most people will follow you because they share your core interests (your 'signal'), but they will rapidly lose interest if too many of your tweets are not relevant to these interests (effectively 'noise' they have to filter out when scanning through their timeline):

- Consider how useful and relevant each tweet is before sending it, to increase the likelihood that your followers find your tweets useful and keep following you
- Ensure the majority of your tweets have hyperlinks to further information

- Provide an image (or video) to accompany your tweets where possible (research by Twitter shows that tweets with images are retweeted 35% more than text-only tweets and videos give a 28% uplift). Bear in mind that some web links automatically generate an accompanying image (e.g. many blogs, newspaper sites and video sites automatically generate an image, title and first line of the article below your tweet once it has been sent)
- Avoid sending too many tweets and retweets at a time — if you're at a conference and tweeting every couple of minutes, followers who aren't interested in the conference are likely to get fed up with you dominating their timeline on a single narrow issue and unfollow you
- Avoid using too many acronyms and abbreviations in your tweets — they may make sense to you but many people reading fast will simply skim over your tweet if they don't understand you instantly. It is better to say less in complete words than to try and cram too much in, if it means you resort to acronyms and abbreviations
- If you're increasingly tweeting about things that are very different from your core interests, consider setting up a new Twitter stream devoted to that issue/interest

- If you're tweeting from a project or institutional account, try not to mix work and personal tweets. Remember you're tweeting on behalf of a group, so telling people about what you're doing on holiday is going to sound a bit strange (either your institution appears to be on holiday or it becomes clear that the Twitter stream is really only about one person (who's on holiday) and not the whole group). If you do want to mix personal and work tweets (some commentators suggest this can help build rapport with your followers), make sure your biography clearly states the name of the person tweeting on behalf of the project or organisation
- Delete conversations once they're finished. One of the great strengths of Twitter is the capacity to join in conversations about your research and other people's work. However, people are less likely to follow you if they look through your timeline and can't find information-rich, relevant material easily because it is cluttered up with lots of conversation. Particularly if you're about to strategically follow a lot of people, make sure you delete all recent replies from your timeline (assuming the conversations are over), so that they can easily see your material and are more likely to follow you It is also worth working on the signal-to-noise ratio in those you follow — if you find that you've started automatically skimming or skipping tweets by certain people, the chances are they rarely have anything particularly relevant/useful to say — unfollow them and reduce the amount of noise you have to put up with.

4. Get your timing right

Because of the way Twitter works, most people only read a fraction of the tweets in their timeline, so if you're tweeting on a day and time that none of your audience are reading their timelines, you could be tweeting into the void (for example, tweeting in the night might be useful if your primary audience is on the other side of the world, but if not, then your tweets will probably be lost deep in your main audience's timelines by the time they wake up and start reading tweets over breakfast). Timing is also about linking to the issues of the day — reframing to link into an ongoing news story or debate can really get your research some attention:
- Link your tweets to ongoing events in academia and the news, using linked hashtags where relevant

- If you've got a lot to say, don't tweet in bursts; rather spread your tweets through the day, using something like HootSuite to automatically schedule your tweets to be sent at different times of the day and week (so you don't have to keep interrupting your day). Someone who only logs onto Twitter at the end of the day may not get to the three tweets you put out at 8 am, but will probably get at least one of the ones that were scheduled for the afternoon. Warning: your friends might think you have super-human powers when they discover you're tweeting while lecturing or speaking at a conference (many people actually schedule conference tweets in advance, based on the programme timings)
- Get to know when your followers are most likely to read your tweets. The time of day you're most likely to get retweets and other engagement from academics is 7–9 am and 5–7 pm on week days, before/after and during the commute to/from work. Tweeting between 8 and 9 am is particularly effective, in my experience. There is often a quite different audience of academics reading tweets at the weekend to these weekday times, so it is worth repeating key messages from the week at the weekend. Similarly, if you come across some great work-related material over the weekend, remember to reuse it later in the week when different people are more likely to pick it up
- Repeat key tweets at different times the following days — if you have a newsletter, set HootSuite to tweet a headline per day with the link to your newsletter PDF
- Have a relatively constant presence if you can — if you only have time to log on once a day or once a week, schedule your tweets to spread them through the day or week.

5. Use Twitter as part of a wider social media and communications strategy

Twitter is just one of many social media platforms, so consider putting your material out via other platforms too, and remember that people who might use your research aren't always using social media, so you're going to want to think about other ways of reaching out to your audiences:
- Come up with a properly thought-through social media strategy as part of a wider communications strategy for your research, whether as an individual, a project or an institution — what are you trying to achieve through communication?

Why are you using social media? Set your goals, come up with a strategy to meet them and monitor your progress
- Everyone has different learning preferences (some like to read, others to listen, watch or do) and everyone has different preferences for the media through which they want to learn. Therefore, try and adapt your research for as many different learning preferences as possible, via as many different media as you have time to engage with. Also tweet links to different types of media — press releases, videos, journal articles, photos etc.
- Adapt your approach to each platform, rather than just linking Twitter to your Facebook account. Effective use of Twitter involves resending key tweets a few times, which is likely to annoy friends on Facebook or colleagues on LinkedIn. Instead, consider setting up a Facebook group for your project or institution, and just putting material there. Alternatively, use the Selective Tweets app on Facebook and choose which tweets you want to appear on Facebook by putting #fb at the end of your tweet.
- Remember that social media is just one form of communication, and that there will be many who are interested in your work who are not using these technologies. Keep up your project newsletter — printing and posting where relevant (but still tweeting the link to the PDF, hosted somewhere you can count hits like Scribd, ResearchGate or ISSUU). Keep presenting at conferences and running workshops for the end users of your research (of course tweeting videos of what you do on You Tube and putting your presentations on SlideShare).

6. Constantly refine your practice

Watch how other academics, projects or institutions with large followings tweet:
- Learn good practice from others, and experiment yourself
- Take note when something annoys you about the way other people use Twitter and avoid doing that yourself

Monitor and learn from your successes and flops:
- Which of your tweets are most likely to get retweeted? Which tweets don't get retweeted? What do they have in common, and what can you learn from this? How were you using Twitter on the day you got 10 new followers?

- Put (open access) documents that you cite on Twitter in places where you can count hits — which tweets make people click on the link (and presumably read your document), and which ones fall flat? What can you learn from this?
- Experiment with different headlines in Twitter to see which ones work best — try and reframe your point and tweet it again later that day, and see if you have more success
- Read through the material you're tweeting and find quotes you can use to promote the link in a slightly different way — sometimes one of these quotes really takes off, far more effectively than the headline. If you're tweeting a blog you wrote, then you might want to consider retitling the blog at this point!

7. Remember it's all about relationships

Don't forget that Twitter is about communicating and building a relationship with people and not just marketing your own or your institution's work at them. So, remember to check other similar institutions'/academics' tweets and respond to those that are interesting. Twitter allows your work to reach a much wider audience and also enables more discussion of your work with others who may put it into practice.

Also, as with any other social setting there is 'Twitter etiquette', for example: thank or favourite mentions about your work; and always give credit where it's due. If someone gave you the information credit him or her with it, either by using "via @person1" (if they are a Twitter user) or as a quote in text.

You Tube: How to turn your research findings into a video that people actually want to watch

It seems that everyone is making videos about their research these days, but if you look at the number of views, not many of these films are actually getting their message across to large audiences. So how do you make a video about your research that people will actually want to watch?

I think there are two crucial things you need to get right which most researchers overlook:

- Come up with a powerful idea that can act as a vehicle for your research findings, for example, a real-life story or a striking, humorous or thought-provoking metaphor. Make your idea personal, unexpected, visually striking and visceral (Box 16)
- Have a strategy in place to drive traffic to your video. Just having a great video isn't enough — people have to know that it is there. For online videos, social media is a powerful means of driving traffic, so make sure you have a social media strategy in place to harness its power to get your film noticed. Find out how to make a social media strategy for your video here.

If you have sufficient budget, hiring a professional film company to make a short video about your key findings can be a powerful and highly professional way to communicate messages to policy audiences, as well as to other key stakeholder groups. If you're working on a much smaller budget and cannot afford to pay for a professional video to be made, you may be surprised at how effective it can be to create your own videos, with just a few tips to help make it come across effectively.

I've got no budget — can I make the film myself?

With the low cost of digital video equipment (and integration of video recorders of sufficient quality for online streaming on most mobile phones nowadays), combined with the ready availability of free and easy-to-use video-editing software (such as Windows Moviemaker™ or Apple's iMovie™), producing your own video content is now within the reach of even the most ardent technophobe. Here are some pointers to make the process easier:

1. Plan thoroughly and write a script — this will ensure you get the shots you want and you don't video more than you need, thus making editing much easier
   a. Spend time thinking about your story, and tell it like a story with a clear beginning, middle and end
   b. Think about how you can make that story personal in some way to the people who will watch your film, which will make them apply your research in some way to their own lives
   c. Try and think of something that will take people by surprise — this is one of the elements of a video that is most likely to make someone share the film with their social network
   d. Try and come up with some memorable visuals e.g. some sort of visual metaphor that sums up your research findings, a spectacular location or something entertaining that will help the key ideas stick in people's heads
   e. Think about how you might be able to engage with people's emotions on some level (ideally positive rather than negative emotions)
2. Turn your script into a 'story board' — little sketches that convey what will happen visually for each section of your script

3. Pay attention to the sound — if possible use an external microphone for interviews, or make sure the speaker is near enough to the camera's built-in microphone, and watch out for background noise.
4. Be aware of what the person in front of the camera is wearing — some colours interfere with the white balance and exposure, especially if you let the camera do it automatically. Avoid pure reds, whites and blacks, dangly or flashy jewellery (usually for women, and this doesn't just interfere with colour but also sound) and complex patterns or stripes
5. Always use a tripod for filming static shots and avoid zooming or moving the camera around unless it is absolutely necessary
6. Make the editing software work for you — use titles, transitions and effects to convey meaning and make your video look more polished, but beware: over-using effects can be distracting and may look unprofessional
7. Get clearance — getting signed consent forms from participants and using only copyright-cleared materials for things like images and soundtracks could save you massive potential headaches later on
8. Make videos available in as many formats as you have time to create in order to improve accessibility (e.g. You Tube, Vimeo, podcast, embedded in your project website, links to download files in .mp4 and .wmv formats)
9. The optimum length of a video on You Tube is said to be between two and three minutes — if you want to keep your audience to the end, try and keep your film within five minutes
10. Keep viewer interest by making videos entertaining where possible, and using a variety of styles, e.g. expert interviews, site visits/tours, documentary, biographical, profiles etc.
11. Also be aware that different styles suit different audiences — just like writing an academic paper and rewording it for a more general audience. So as mentioned below with professional film-makers, try and do a shortened, more general version of your video, one for the academic (the specialist audience) and one for your stakeholders. It may be a good idea, especially if you are tight on budget or time, that you do one film, which can be used for both. This may need a little bit of extra planning and adjusting your own way of speaking, especially using simple language to convey your message. Even academics will key into your video if you

185

choose your words wisely and the content is relevant, has a story, is entertaining and visually pleasing or visceral (Box 16)

12. Attempt to make videos look as professional as possible, e.g. by adding introductory and end titles/credits

13. Promote your video — just putting a video online won't necessarily get you any views. You need to integrate your video into your project's pathway to impact and think of ways to drive traffic to it. Just embedding it in your project website won't help if you're not getting much traffic to your website. It can be particularly useful to invest in social media to drive traffic to online videos

14. Have a go! Learn by doing it and get constructive feedback from your colleagues, but don't be too ambitious on your first attempt.

How do I get the most out of a professional film-maker?

Most of the points above apply when commissioning a video, except that the professionals will take care of much of this for you. Here are a few key pointers that can help you get the most out of working with film-makers:

- Although many film-makers will be able to help you refine your story, you will still need to provide them with the source material. Given that you understand your research best, you can often get much better results if you come to a film-maker with a few different ideas about how you might tell your story, that they can then work with, rather than just sending them your latest paper or policy brief and hoping that they'll be able to come up with the story on their own

- Think about who you'll need to interview and what locations you'd like to film — every extra day of filming on location adds to your budget, so if you can get everyone in the same place on your key location, you may be able to get filming days down to a minimum and save on costs

- Once you know what you want from the film, you can negotiate a price — there will be an element of give and take, and you may have to scale back your ambitions depending on your budget

- Ask the film-maker if they can provide a cut-down 'promotional' version of your film within the price or for a small additional fee — this can be an effective way of

186

creating an additional version of your film that may be more relevant for a more generalist audience, to help expand who accesses your material

- Make sure you check the draft version of your film carefully and provide detailed comments about things that need to be changed. Take time at this point and consult with the rest of your team, rather than going back and forth with lots of edits, or colleagues objecting to content after the film is finished
- Get copies of your film in a few different formats — lower resolution for putting online and higher resolution for showing on the big screen.

LinkedIn for research impact

LinkedIn is a little more limited in its potential for research impact, but can be used in certain ways to support your work, for example:

- Connect with stakeholders from organisations you would like to work with to deliver impact. Use the features in the advanced search on LinkedIn — it is a surprisingly powerful search engine, enabling you to focus (for example) on their

location, the company they work for or industry they are in. You don't have to have worked with them before to be able to connect with them. Use your current job title in your connection request, and if necessary Google them to find their email address, and include a short note with your contact request (rather than just using the default message), explaining that you're interested in their work and think they might be interested in your research (you'll get a much better acceptance rate this way)

- Once you've got connections with a good range of stakeholders, create status updates and blogs on LinkedIn specifically related to the impacts you want to achieve. In this way, you are starting to put your work in front of people so they become more familiar with it and are more likely to trust you as a credible source of information and help
- Find LinkedIn groups talking about issues linked to your research, request to join and contribute to the discussion before adding in links to your work
- After some time of generating content, start interacting with your LinkedIn contacts by sending them messages about your work. These go straight to their email inbox and they can reply from their email, so its easy for people to respond to you. According to your social media strategy and impact plan, you should have a clear goal in mind when you are reaching out to people. Ask yourself what you want to achieve and what they will gain from interacting with you.

Twitter, You Tube and LinkedIn are, of course, just three out of a rapidly growing range of social media platforms you can choose from. From my own experience and the experience of those I've trained, however, these are the best suited to driving impact from research. If you want to see how I use these platforms so we can learn together, don't be shy — search for my name on LinkedIn or follow @fasttrackimpact on Twitter.

Chapter 18
How to crowdfund your research to engage with the public

As research funding from traditional sources becomes increasingly competitive, many researchers are now turning to the public to directly fund their work. However, with these new opportunities come a number of pitfalls, so you will need to think carefully about whether or not your research is suited to this approach. For me, one of the most exciting things about the crowdfunding model is the way that it drives engagement with your research, helping people understand what you're doing to a depth that is rarely possible through other forms of online engagement.

Crowdfunding websites like Kickstarter and IndieGogo are increasingly funding projects in technology, the arts, campaigns and non-profit community work, with some projects raising significant sums of money. Projects listed on these crowdfunding websites offer investors a range of rewards, based on the amount they are willing to invest, with small rewards available for as little as a £1 investment, rising to personalised products and events to reward larger investments.

Now a number of websites have started to offer opportunities to invest in research, for example, experiment.com and RocketHub. These initiatives are less about getting your hands on the latest gadget before it hits the shops, and more based on the warm glow of knowing you've advanced knowledge and made the world a better place. Having said this, many projects do offer personal rewards.

Crowdfunding research involves raising money directly from the public, with the research project idea articulated on a dedicated project page along with an invitation for individuals to help fund it. Typically the project only goes ahead once the funding target has been reached, and only at that point are supporter's payments actually taken. Depending on the platform you are using and the way you set up your project, you may still be able to take funds that are pledged if you do not reach your target, but you will need to be able

189

Q Search Projects, Topics & Lab Notes

Discover   How It Works   Sign up or Login

Help fund the next wave of scientific research

Start an Experiment | Browse Projects

"This solution helps close the gap for potential and promising, but unfunded projects."
Bill Gates

★ **Featured Experiments**

Bringing you the freshest daily servings of science.

Comprehensive Conservation of Southern Resident Killer Whales in the Modern Ocean

Southern Resident Killer Whales are endangered; only 85 remain. In today's modern ocean they face many threats simultaneously.

Ecology   Social Science

 Lindsey Peavey
University of California, Santa

| 49% funded | $4,000 goal | 29 days left |

Lost in the mountains: Describing new species in the High Atlas Mountains of Morocco

Biodiversity is not evenly distributed on the planet, but is concentrated in hotspots with high conservation value. Identifying...

Biology   Earth Science

 Joana Rodrigues Lopes dos S...
University of Porto

| 30% funded | $1,400 goal | 2 days left |

Digital preservation of immaterial island culture in the face of climate change

In island states around the world, living culture is under threat. Climate change, globalization, increased migration...

Computer Science   Social Science

 Island Ark Project Team
Various Universities and the De...

| 65% funded | $3,900 goal | 2 days left |

---

to deliver project outcomes, including rewards, with whatever money you raise.

What sort of projects are likely to get crowdfunded?

The answer to this question depends upon the sort of project you want to fund. If it will lead to a technology, product, experience, performance or some other tangible output that members of the public may want to own or experience, then the chances are that you may be onto a winner. A successful crowdfunded project needs to be beautifully and effectively presented and explained, making it clear how it will make a difference. You'll need a strategy to drive people to your project page and get them interested enough to read about what you plan to research (blogging, tweeting, getting traditional media coverage etc.). To attract visitors, many crowdfunded projects offer affordable and desirable rewards to investors.

Most crowdfunded research projects are relatively small, requiring a few hundred or thousand pounds. Therefore, current crowdfunding of research is often used for 'seed-corn' funding bigger projects, testing ideas and prototypes, which can then attract larger amounts of funding from more traditional research funding sources. However, with a bit of clever project design, researchers can 'think big' when using crowdfunding, and divide projects into self-contained work packages that can function effectively on their own. Then, if more than one work package is funded, they will link together to form a larger, longer-term project.

Importantly for us as researchers, crowdfunding our work can also open the doors to better public engagement and communication. Crowdfunding platforms represent an emerging form of collaboration between researchers and those who use our research, where the public can be informed and inform the research process. For example, FundaGeek enables discussion forums where the public can debate the value of a project alongside any moral concerns.

Tips for a successful crowdfunding campaign

If you think you've got an idea that might fit the crowdfunding model, then here are a few tips that will help you make your research idea become a reality:

191

1. Take a look at successfully funded projects to get inspiration for the sorts of rewards you might be able to offer investors, from highly affordable options to more expensive options for larger investors. We recommend that you look at projects that have been successful in areas with a longer history of crowdfunding e.g. technology, charity and the arts, to get ideas about what works
2. Purge your project of all jargon, so you can communicate your project in a way that excites and inspires people to fund you — something most researchers need to practise
3. Creating a slick video to promote the project is a must, to make it as accessible as possible to potential investors (many crowdfunding websites require this anyway). Make sure your presentation and message is personal, visual, original/unexpected and, if possible, appeals to people at an emotional level (Box 16)
4. Set a realistic funding goal, dividing large projects into self-contained, smaller projects (effectively work packages) that are more likely to get funded
5. Pay particular attention to creating a social media strategy with clear aims to promote your campaign (Chapter 16). Systematically consider who your audience is, their preferences and interests, the sorts of media and communications they are most likely to respond to, and the offer/reward that people in your audience are likely to respond to. Build your social media following before you launch your campaign, and think about how to target people who are well connected to your target audience (e.g. large Twitter followings), so they can promote your campaign for you. Promote your project as widely as possible via social media, and then via your personal and professional networks.

What problems might I encounter?

There are a number of practical and ethical challenges to crowdfunding research. First, not all investors may honour their pledges, and so the eventual sum raised may fall short of the target. Although websites take payment details electronically from investors, credit checks are often performed many months prior to the end of the campaign when payments are actually taken. This may mean it is not possible to fulfil your commitments to those who do honour their pledges, and in the worst case scenario they may demand refunds or sue the project.

Second, not all crowdfunding platforms have a peer-review or ethics review process to screen projects before they go online. We can all think of projects that we thought were watertight when we submitted them, that came back from peer-review or ethics review with fundamental problems that meant they were unfundable. In this case, you may discover these fundamental flaws only once you've started spending on the project, and may not be able to bring it to completion. Even worse, such projects may inadvertently put members of the public at risk and lead to unintended consequences. Take a look at the policies of different crowdfunding websites, and use sites that have some sort of review process. This will also mean your project isn't sitting beside pseudo-science projects that you would not want to be associated with. Particularly useful are sites that include discussion forums where you can engage with potential investors to debate the validity and ethics of what you are doing. In this way, engaging with crowdfunding actually has the potential to enhance the quality of the research you develop. It is also always wise to get feedback from friendly colleagues before you submit anything for funding, whether to traditional funders or a crowdfunding website.

Third, some people worry about the fact that you have no way of vetting the people who fund your research, or knowing if they may have a conflict of interest — for subjects where you have to declare your funders and any conflicts of interest as part of the publication process. Although this is something to think about, I have not heard of any projects that have fallen foul of this at publication stage, and there is a contrary argument that the number of different people funding your research immediately demonstrates the perceived value and likely impact of your work.

Finally, before going down this route, make sure you check with the funding office in your institution if they are able to accept crowdfunding for your research, or allow you to accept this funding for research conducted under their auspices.

So should I crowdfund my next research project?

Obviously it depends on the type of project you are trying to fund, and how easily you think it will resonate with the public. The answer

193

will depend to a large extent on the sort of research field you are working in, and the likely risks of the project going wrong, either in terms of the research itself or health and safety. It might feel risky to try this for the first time, but why not start small with a low-risk, low-cost project that can lay the ground for something more ambitious later?

This new funding model may be particularly attractive to early career academics and those who are good at communicating their research to the public. Unlike many traditional funders who require you to have a permanent or 'tenured' academic post before they'll even look at your funding application, anyone can apply for crowdfunding. You can potentially be up and running with your new project in a few months, compared to the long and drawn-out traditional review process, giving you the platform you need for the bigger projects that will get you greater job security. Crowdfunding may also be increasingly popular with more established researchers, who are seeking new ways to engage with the likely users of their work and generate impact, given funders' increasing focus on the impact agenda.

Crowdfunding research is in its early stages. It is therefore unsurprising that its many potential benefits have largely been overlooked by the research community. This approach isn't all about getting money for research; it is a new way of doing research in collaboration with your funders —the public — giving you an instant route to public engagement in your work. For me, crowdfunding is about the democratisation of science and making sure your research resonates with the wider interests and needs of society.

Chapter 19
How to engage policy-makers with research: a relational approach

Working with policy-makers is one way that you can achieve impacts of national and even global scale. While we can all create policy briefs easily enough (see the next chapter for tips on how to create policy briefs that have real impact), actually having influence on policy is a real challenge. Depending on the country where you would like to have policy impacts, there may be very different protocols for accessing politicians and members of the civil service. In some countries, there are no official routes to get evidence into policy (this typically applies to countries that do not operate democracies, though some democracies do a good job of hiding these routes). In these cases, your pathway to policy impact may be via powerful Non-Governmental Organisations and other people who can influence policy in other ways.

The aim of this chapter isn't to give you a detailed guide to the political apparatus of any particular country — for that you will need to look elsewhere. Instead, the aim here is to consider how you, as a researcher, can make your evidence accessible to policy-makers in an engaging and influential way. The word 'influence' in this context is problematic for many researchers, but if we want to take a relational approach to impact, I believe that it isn't enough to simply post a policy brief. The reality is that the majority of people in the policy community call on trusted advisors for advice relating to research evidence, and are less likely to listen to evidence from sources they do not trust. Just having your paper published in a top journal isn't enough to engender trust and be listened to. You need to demonstrate your credibility and trustworthiness in the context of a long-term relationship with key members of the policy community and become embedded in that community if you really want to be listened to.

I believe that one of the most effective ways of achieving policy change is through a 'pincer' movement of influence from the bottom up and the top down. It is usually easiest to start from the bottom up, connecting with policy analysts and government researchers who have a similar background to you, and who are likely to easily understand the research and where you are coming from. Starting by building strong, trusting relationships with more junior civil servants, you can begin to understand which of their managers has relevant interests and influence, and begin to introduce them to your ideas too.

However, this approach can only go so far if the minister is not aware of the work. Getting access to a minister is a rare opportunity for most researchers, so you may need to rely on intermediaries such as charities or others who have existing relationships and routes to those in power. I've discussed some of the ethical dilemmas that this poses for researchers below. If you can present a case for policy change based on your evidence (even if second hand via an intermediary), and convince (and perhaps inspire) a senior policy-maker that they should take action, then it is important that they are met with informed civil servants when they take the idea to their team. If their team hasn't heard of your work, doesn't trust you and isn't convinced by the case as it is put to them by the minister (which may not be how you would have put it to them), they may raise so many questions and doubts that your ideas are dismissed as unworkable. On the other hand, if the minister is met with informed judgements from civil servants who are already aware of your work, and have critically examined it, there is a much higher chance that change will occur. Equally, just convincing civil servants that your research deserves attention may not be enough if it doesn't fit with the interests and priorities of the minister at that time. So taking both the top-down and bottom-up route are, I believe, important if you really want to effect change. Box 17 provides a few questions that can help you design your own 'pincer' movement for evidence-informed policy change.

How should I start?

The first step is to identify the key messages from your research that are likely to be relevant to current or future policy, and why these messages are important. This is often an iterative process, researching the policy environment and getting feedback from people in the policy community, to help you focus on the most relevant aspects of your research and frame clear messages that are likely to resonate with the issues and challenges they face. This initial feedback may be via social (or other) media or via people at the periphery of the policy community e.g. researchers who have a long

196

track record of working with the policy community in your field, government researchers or agency staff. It is better to get constructive feedback from these people to have a polished, concise and relevant pitch ready for those who are likely to have greater influence.

If you are working on a fairly narrow topic (a common problem for PhD students who want to work with the policy community), it can be hard to make your work relevant enough to warrant attention from busy policy analysts. However, if you are able to make connections between your work and the work of colleagues, and contextualise this within the latest research findings that link your narrow research topic to the bigger picture, then it may become easier to reach these audiences. Although your research may now be relegated to a box or a paragraph and accompanying figure, at least there is a good chance that people will engage with your research now.

Consider exactly what you might want a policy-maker to do with the knowledge you are providing — make sure it is something that is actually achievable, and if it isn't, then work out what the initial steps might be towards the action you'd want to see in the longer term. There is evidence that research findings that build on rather than break down existing policies are more likely to be adopted — recommendations for a series of incremental changes rather than a single-step change are more likely to be adopted. Having said this, sometimes it may be as important to enable an individual or organisation to 'unlearn' certain accepted concepts and ways of doing things (such as the accepted health effects of a particular food or lifestyle choice) in order to take on board new understanding based on the latest research (e.g. suggesting that what we previously thought was healthy may have negative consequences for health).

Box 17: Designing a pincer movement for evidence-informed policy change

1. Identify policy stakeholders from your stakeholder analysis (see Chapter 13 and template in Part 4). Check that you are being as specific as possible: which policy area, department, or team are you identifying that may be interested in your research?
2. Identify areas of policy that may be related to or similar to your research in some way:
    a. Can you link your research to these live policy debates in some way? Would the insights from your research enrich these debates?
    b. If so, who would you need to collaborate with to connect to these wider debates?
    c. If not, what future work might you do that could contribute to these debates? What could you do now to start this work?
3. Top-down influence:
    a. What other organisations are working in this policy area to influence policy?
    b. Which of these do you think has most influence?
    c. What are the key messages from your research that are likely to be of most interest to them?
    d. Can you find out more about their priorities and modes of operation, and start to get to know people in the organisation who will be interested in your work?
4. Bottom-up influence:
    a. What evidence teams within the civil service are working on the policy debates you can connect to?
    b. Can you make a policy brief that is relevant enough to secure you a meeting with someone junior?
    c. If not, can you get introduced by someone who they already know and trust (look through your network and those of your colleagues and work out what you could do for the person who might introduce you)

      d.   Once you have a contact within Government, find out from them what the evidence gaps are that they need to fill and offer to help

      e.   Stay in regular touch and build trust, asking questions that will enable you to work out who in their team and wider network has most influence. Find out the events that these people go to and try to connect with them there so they know who you are and what you're doing before you are introduced to them by their own colleagues

      f.   Gradually connect your research with people of increasing influence via departmental seminars and one-to-one meetings

5.   Plan for your impacts

      a.   Go back to your impact plan (Chapter 9 and template in Part 4) and revise your activities and timings for engaging with policy stakeholders

One of the greatest challenges of constructing messages from your research is how to communicate complexity and uncertainty clearly, without putting off policy-makers who want clear answers. It is important to avoid giving a false sense of certainty e.g. via numbers, graphs or maps that hide variability, error bars or alternative scenarios. However, case studies, stories and personalised findings can help communicate complexity and bring the key points home to decision-makers. A common problem that members of the policy community have with researchers is our propensity to selectively promote our own latest research, overlooking equally valuable and often highly complementary work by other researchers that could significantly increase the value of our own research for policy-makers. By summarising other research on the topic, you may also be able to reduce uncertainty and increase the credibility of your own research by showing the range and depth of research that backs up your claims.

It can often pay dividends to work with professional communicators (e.g. science writers, knowledge brokers, your institute public relations officers and/or film-makers) to translate your work into terms that can be understood by those you want to influence. Also knowledge brokers can help facilitate your dialogue with policy-makers, helping you 'translate' discipline-specific language and mediate if needed.

When should I engage?

The best time to engage is at the start of every research project. After you have identified your 'target audience' you need to find out if these groups really do find it relevant for their work. Together, you will then be able to formulate research questions that are relevant for both of you. By doing this, everyone involved knows what outcomes are likely to arise from the research (and when), and potential uncertainties can already start to be communicated at this stage.

There are certain times when a piece of evidence may be crucial in policy decisions. It is therefore important to be in regular contact with members of the policy community, so that you can easily identify those key moments and changing demands. If they already know you, they're likely to come to you for the answers. Even if that means that you are being asked for evidence before the research has been completed, remember that you have a much broader knowledge base than the project you are currently working on, which could still enable you to link to existing published evidence to help provide the answers that are needed. In some cases, it may be possible to provide preliminary findings, as long as the limitations and uncertainties are made clear. New political leadership in a particular government department or agency can be a problem (in terms of continuity), or in fact may become an opportunity to present new ideas to leaders looking for new ways of achieving their goals. Working with political parties to get your ideas into election manifestos can be an effective way of getting research into policy, if you don't feel too uncomfortable about appearing to be affiliated with a particular party.

Where should I engage?

The majority of key players are extremely busy, and you need to consider how to bring your message to them. Most government departments and agencies will host seminars if you can demonstrate that your research is of great enough relevance, for example, by bringing together a number of key experts to present their research alongside yours. You can also hire a venue near to the Parliament and offer a free lunch to incentivise attendance. However, for many of the most important players, you may need to arrange a short face-to-face appointment with them or their close advisors, to get your message across. Many politicians are active on social media, and this can be an easy way to get their initial attention and start to build relationships with them.

To engage with policy-makers on international policy matters, you will need to explore events and bodies relevant to your work, such as the UN Convention of Biological Diversity and its associated Subsidiary Body of Technical and Technological Advice. Remember, it is these technical events where many decisions are typically made and where you have greatest influence as a researcher, rather than the larger, better-publicised events which the high-profile politicians attend. Some countries have set up specific science-policy interfaces or platforms, to enhance dialogue between researchers and policy-makers. It is be worth checking if one exists for your given research area.

Identifying who has the power to affect policy change

Using stakeholder analysis (Chapters 9 and 13), it should be possible to identify organisations and key individuals within those organisations who are particularly influential, who you might want to try and build relationships with. These may be policy-makers themselves, or it may be the advisors who work closely with them within the civil service. It is important not to overlook organisations and individuals outside the policy community who have long-standing relationships with key members of the policy community and may have a lot of influence, for example, from Non-Governmental Organisations, charities, think tanks, business and lobby groups.

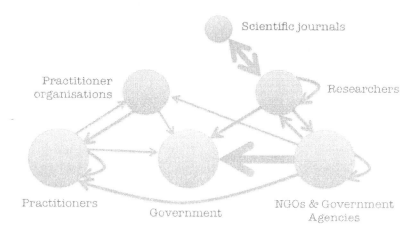

Figure 12: Simplified representation of a Social Network Analysis, showing how peatland research reaches policy-makers. Circles represent different sources or users of knowledge, with larger circles more likely to provide/receive knowledge than smaller circles. Arrows show flows of knowledge from one source to another, with the thickness of the arrow proportional to the number of times communication of research findings occurred between sources.

Where possible, identify 'boundary organisations' that are able to cross boundaries between otherwise disconnected networks of actors, including researchers and policy-makers. There will often be key individuals within these organizations who understand the research and are well connected to and trusted by the policy community, who may be able to help you engage credibly with their contacts. If you understand who has influence, you can start to identify the messages from your research that are likely to resonate with these influencers and develop a communication strategy that will enable you to build relationships with these key people, who will then open doors to the policy community for you.

A few years ago, I decided to try and trace how research was getting into policy and practice (or not), and my colleagues and I chose 77 different research findings and traced how they travelled from peer-reviewed literature into policy and practice through social networks using social network analysis and interviews with those who had found out about the research, to see how they learned about it and who they had passed it onto. One of those findings was the work on peatland carbon that I'd been involved with, and Figure 12 is a simplified representation of the network map showing how that research got into policy and practice. It shows how peatland researchers tend to mainly communicate their findings through scientific journals, which are not used directly as a major source of knowledge by policy-makers or those who seek to influence them. On the other hand, researchers in this case were as good at communicating their findings to NGOs and charities as to policy-makers directly, and it was through these NGOs and charities that most of the information reached the government.

This presents an interesting dilemma for researchers. Charities and lobby groups have more time and resources to promote research findings that support their causes than researchers typically have, but they have an incentive to present a selective or biased representation of the research. Again, this often comes down to relationships. Although it is impossible to control how others represent our research, by engaging with these knowledge brokers, it is possible to increase the likelihood that they fully understand our research, including important nuances, caveats and remaining uncertainties. If you can create a strong, trusting relationship with key people in these groups, they are more likely to keep you informed of the way they are using your work, and respond proactively if you spot problems with the way they are using it.

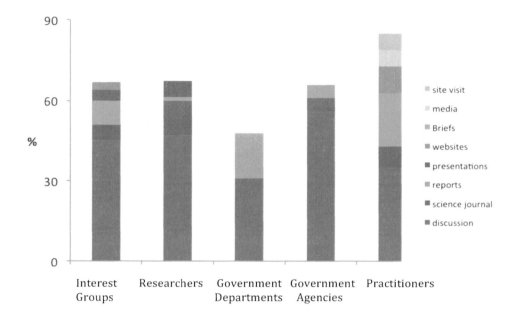

Figure 13: Case study research showing how different groups find out about new research findings, based on interviews in Scotland as part of the Ecocycles project.

How to build relationships with policy-makers

Relationships are at the core of my approach to working with policy-makers. My own research and other published evidence shows that although policy-makers find out about research from many sources, it is information from face-to-face contact with people they trust that most commonly influences decisions (Figure 13). It doesn't matter whether it is a one-to-one meeting or at a workshop, conference or seminar, and it doesn't matter if the contact is directly with the researcher or more indirectly via some sort of intermediary, for example, someone from a Government agency or a charity or lobbying group. The important thing for researchers is to invest time in developing trusting, two-way relationships with key members of the policy community working in their field.

Although Figure 13 is based on just one case study, the key points appear again and again in the literature: policy-makers find out about much of the research they use through face-to-face contact with trusted sources. The graph above shows that although the interest groups and agencies advising and lobbying Government do use journal papers as a source of knowledge, they are far outweighed by face-to-face communication with trusted sources. Although they do use policy briefs, again, face-to-face discussion with trusted sources is the most important way they find out about research evidence. Creating a policy brief is not enough: it is what you do with your policy brief that counts. Leaving a policy brief as a reminder of key points and a link to further information after a face-to-face meeting with someone is far more likely to effect change than simply mailing out briefs and hoping someone reads them.

Finally, it is important to consider how you will demonstrate the credibility of your message, when you're not going to have time to present all the methods and data that lie behind it. In many cases, this credibility can be earned by proxy, by referencing a key paper in a prestigious journal that your findings are based on, and by being introduced under the brand of your funders or by key figures who are already trusted by the policy community.

Influencing policy

In the world of politics, emotion is often used to bias decisions away from the evidence. Many researchers prize their objectivity and detached independence. However, positive, effectively channelled emotion gets people's attention — it makes people sit up and take notice. Using emotion appropriately, as researchers, we can connect with our audience and engender empathy. By engaging with both hearts and minds, we increase the likelihood that our audience is really listening, and actively considering how our evidence fits with the other evidence they have access to, their goals and their worldview.

As experts, we hold a privileged position of authority, which is likely to be a key factor in getting us an audience with decision-makers in the first place. Retaining that credibility is essential, and so it is important to carefully channel our emotions. Decision-makers are more likely to respond to positive emotion than they are to anger, or doom and gloom predictions. For example, there is evidence that decision-makers are less receptive to messages about the value of nature if these messages are perceived as threatening their psychological needs of autonomy (e.g. because they feel manipulated or coerced), happiness (e.g. environmental and sexual health campaigns based on fear), reputation (e.g. because they feel implicitly criticised or patronised) and self-esteem (e.g. because they start to feel responsible for or guilty about the issues concerned). On the other hand, enthusiasm is infectious. Presenting our evidence with passion and crafting our arguments to meet the innate psychological needs of our audience is more likely to get people to listen, even if they don't act on what they hear.

Implicit. so far, is the idea that the evidence itself is unquestionable; the question is only whether we as researchers should use emotion to communicate that evidence. But there are many researchers who would challenge the idea that research is (or can ever be) entirely independent, emotionally detached and objective. If we recognise that our research is just one strand of evidence feeding into what are usually political decision-making processes, then we can begin to explore the subjectivity inherent in many of the processes we use to generate 'evidence', and can become less detached and more emotionally engaged in the normative goals that pervade our work.

Traditionally, the mass media has been an important way of amplifying messages, so policy-makers receive our messages from many different sources and are given a sense of the weight of public opinion behind that message. Nowadays, social media is an increasingly important way of amplifying messages in a more relational way, raising awareness of the issues we're working on and demonstrating wider public support for our ideas very transparently via counts of retweets, likes and views. Whether you're using social media or not, developing a partnership or 'policy network' with other individuals and organisations who are interested in the messages arising from your work can also help amplify your message, getting your research to different members of the policy community in different ways (these approaches are considered in more detail in the previous section). Importantly, it is often possible to directly engage with members of the policy community around these messages via social media, enabling you to persuade rather than simply using the pressure of the mass media. Of course, in many cases, having visibility in both mass and social media can further amplify your message.

Practical tips for influencing policy through relationships:

1. **Develop a structured and systematic engagement strategy.** It doesn't have to be written down; even if it is only in your head, thinking systematically about how you will engage with key stakeholders can significantly improve your chances of being relevant and helpful. First of all, map your stakeholders to work out who actually holds decision-making power within an organisation. Often, people with high levels of personal and transpersonal power have greater ability to actually make things happen in an organisation than the people at the top of the hierarchy. Also beware of automatically gravitating to the 'usual suspects' who are highly visible, and consider whether there are marginalised and powerless individuals or groups that could really benefit from your work, and who may be highly motivated to work with you. Once you've worked out who you want to engage with, you need to work out what's likely to motivate them to engage with you. What messages from your research might resonate with their interests and agendas? What modes of communication are they most comfortable with? What is the best timing/occasion for communication? What sort of language do they use or avoid? If you can't reach those with decision-making power to start with, identify people in the organisation who are more likely to engage with you, and expand your network from there. Those with decision-making power are more likely to listen to you if the rest of their team are already listening to you.
2. **Empathise**: put yourself in the other person's shoes; work out what motivates them, how they might be feeling, and what they might want from your research. Work out what is likely to build trust in the relationship between you. For example, do you need a letter-headed initial approach or do you need to be introduced over a pint of beer? It may be worth doing some digging about the person and their organisation, to help you empathise effectively. For example, you might research them online, looking at their profile and the sorts of things they're writing or tweeting about. Alternatively you might ask what others in your network know about them. If none of these ideas work, you can talk to other people in similar roles first, to get a feel for the sorts of issues that are likely to motivate them, and the language and modes of communication they're likely to respond best to.

It's a bit like the sort of process an actor or actress would go through to research a role they've been given.

3. **Practise your communication skills**: find out about body language, so you can read how the people you want to influence are reacting to you and adjust your approach accordingly. Adopt confident body language. If possible, practise in front of a camera or mirror or get feedback from a colleague. You need to practise open body language that tells the other person you trust them and that they can trust you (e.g. avoid crossed arms and legs and give plenty of eye contact). Think about your handshake and what it conveys — a firm handshake conveys confidence and is more likely to instil trust than a limp one. Put your pen down when you're not writing and make sure there are no physical barriers between you (e.g. a pad of paper propped up between you). Be mentally aware of your facial expressions, to make sure you're not slipping into a scowl as you concentrate on what the other person is saying; try and be as smiley as comes naturally to you. It is important to make it clear you're listening and genuinely valuing what they tell you with nods and non-verbal, encouraging sounds. If you're really listening with all your heart, you'll find yourself naturally mirroring the other person to an extent. For example, if you make a strident start and discover the other person is very quiet and shyly spoken, you'll probably feel uncomfortable continuing to talk loudly and confidently, and will moderate your behaviour to be less different from them. If you are able to adapt your tone of voice and body language to theirs, they are likely to feel respected and more able to connect with you. If all of this doesn't come naturally, start small and build from there. Like other roles you have to adopt professionally (e.g. lecturing), with practice it will become second nature, and evntually become entirely natural.

4. **Give**: ensure there genuinely is something in the engagement for the other person that they really want, and think about how you'll deliver those benefits in concrete terms in the near future. If you've managed to really empathise with them, then this bit should be easy.

5. **Assess your power**: assess your power in context of the stakeholders you want to work with, bearing in mind that you may be significantly more or less powerful in different contexts (see Box 12). For example, in some contexts, as a result of negative experience with other researchers, your status as an academic might mean people expect you to be

irrelevant or exploitative. On the other hand, with a different group of stakeholders, your status as an academic might mean your view carries greater weight. One way of thinking about how powerful you might be in a particular context is to think about your levels of:

- Situational power (e.g. your level in formal hierarchies, access to decision-makers)
- Social power (e.g. your social standing, race, marital status or whether you have Dr or Professor in front of your name)
- Personal power (e.g. how charismatic, trustworthy and empathetic you are perceived to be)
- Transpersonal power (e.g. a connection to something larger than yourself, ability to transcend past hurts, freedom from fear and commitment to an altruistic vision)
- If you don't have enough power or legitimacy yourself, then think about ways you might be able to improve your personal and transpersonal power (as these are easier to change than your social and situational power). And if you need a quick shortcut to more power, get yourself introduced or be accompanied by someone who is already well trusted and perceived to be legitimate in the eyes of the people you want to work with. You can assess your own levels of power using the prompts in Box 12

6. Finally, where necessary, **go around or above obstructive individuals**, developing a tailored engagement strategy for the next person in the organisation you need to engage. If you have done everything you can to adapt to the needs and priorities of someone who is preventing you from reaching those with decision-making power in an organisation, see if you can find others in the organisation who have slightly different needs and priorities, or a different world view or perception of risk, and see if they will open a door to decision-makers on your behalf instead. Some individuals are naturally more likely to be receptive to new ideas (they are 'early adopters' of innovations) and others (sometimes termed 'laggards') lag behind and wait for others to try new ideas first. You need to identify the innovators in the organisation you're trying to influence. In a few rare cases,

there may be a case for going to someone higher in the hierarchy. For example, a Minister might see a political opportunity in a high-risk idea emerging from research that their civil servants might not have been willing to consider. However, under instruction from the Minister, civil servants are likely to be happy to investigate your ideas.

Sustaining trusting relationships

Where possible, get feedback on your interactions with policy-makers, whether directly (e.g. via feedback forms after a workshop) or indirectly from colleagues' observations of your interactions. Seek out colleagues and peers from your discipline who are already successfully working with policy-makers on related issues, and learn from them. They will be able to advise on the key people to communicate with, and how best to approach each person. If possible, take opportunities to watch colleagues who have experience of collaborating with policy-makers at work. You can also study

examples of successful (and unsuccessful) policy uptake of similar research. By understanding the factors that led to (or prevented) policy uptake, you may then be able to identify mechanisms you can use or avoid yourself. Although research project funding typically comes to an end after between three and five years, it is important to find ways to sustain engagement with the policy community long after a project ends, if your research is to really make an impact. Only over sustained engagement is it possible to develop trust. It is these trusting relationships that will get you the ear of policy-makers, and enable you to adapt your research to their needs. Finally, be tenacious: put the same effort into building relationships with the latest civil servants to move into the roles you need to work with, again and again...

Top pathways to policy according to researchers

I'd like to conclude with a perspective from researchers who have worked with policy-makers, on the key pathways that enabled them to effect change. In 2015, the Higher Education Funding Council for England published a searchable database of impact case studies, collected as part of its evaluation of UK research under their Research Excellence Framework. I commissioned an analysis of a 5% sample of impacts on social (including health), economic and environmental policy, and classified the different pathways to impact that the researchers identified (you can read the full results in the table below). The most commonly cited impact pathways make interesting reading:

1.   **Publications**: as you might expect, the number one pathway described by researchers in their case studies was academic publications, typically in peer-reviewed journals. Given that most case studies contained multiple pathways, the role that academic publications played in achieving impact is debatable. Also in the top ten pathways, however, were industry publications and policy briefs, underlining the importance of translating academic findings into formats that are more likely to be read by non-academics.

2.   **Advisory roles**: being asked to contribute to Government inquiries, reports, panels and committees was one of the most important ways that researchers influenced policy, with over 50% of the case studies we reviewed using this pathway.

3. **Media coverage**: researchers perceived that getting their research covered in the mass media was an important route to policy impact. This might be because of the visibility that media coverage can afford research, putting it directly in front of decision-makers who engage with the media (themselves or because they are made aware of media coverage by their civil servants), or more indirectly by contributing to a body of public opinion that decision-makers then respond to.

4. **Partnerships and collaborations** with industry and NGOs: by finding organisations that shared their research interests, researchers may have been able to harness the lobbying power of these organisations to promote their work more actively and at higher levels than they would have had the time, resources and ability to do as researchers on their own. These partnerships also enabled researchers to test their research in real-life situations, which gave it more credibility when approaching policy-makers.

5. **Presentations** with industry, the public and Government: face-to-face meetings, whether one-to-one or in workshops and conferences, can be a powerful way to get research findings noticed and understood, partly because the audience has the opportunity to question the research team. Although researchers cited presentations directly to Government, they were just as likely to cite presentations to industry and the public as their pathway to policy impacts. This may suggest, like the previous point, that many impacts were achieved via the knowledge brokerage role of industry partners, or by raising the public profile and contributing towards a weight of public opinion that policy-makers could not ignore.

6. **Developing easily accessible online materials** based on the research was also a commonly cited pathway to policy impact. Although this is rapidly changing with open access, a significant proportion of research findings (particularly older material) is behind journal paywalls. Making this material both available and easily accessible via online materials that translate the findings for specific audiences can be an important way of getting research into policy.

One of the most important pathways was advisory roles. Although these roles are sometimes one-off interactions, for example, giving evidence to a parliamentary committee, many are medium to long-term roles over a period of years, in which the researchers are able to build trust with other panel/committee members and provide advice on an ad hoc basis between formal meetings. Apart from this,

213

however, the majority of the main pathways were in dissemination mode. Although partnerships and collaborations with industry and NGOs feature strongly in the pathways reported by researchers in these case studies, these organisations appear to primarily have operated as knowledge brokers, helping to translate and amplify messages arising from the research, and enabling them to reach policy-makers.

It is clear from the case studies we reviewed that well-targeted dissemination of research findings can pay dividends, but if the experience of these researchers is anything to go by, certain types of dissemination may be more likely to achieve impact, for example, publications, online resources, press releases and presentations. But it is just as important to invest in longer-term relationships with the policy community and key players who have the time, resources and expertise to help you form those relationships and amplify your message. In the long term, this may open up opportunities to contribute to advisory committees and other processes that directly feed into the policy process.

Chapter 20
How to make a policy brief that has real impact

Have you ever wondered if the policy briefs you've produced actually made a difference? There are many guides that will tell you how to write an effective policy brief, but is the wording and design what makes the difference? Well, partly. If you want to make an impact, writing the brief is just a small part of the work. A policy brief is only worth what you do with it.

There are four elements to creating a policy brief that has real impact, and writing and designing the brief is only one of them:
1. Design and planning
2. Writing and feedback loops
3. Distribution
4. Engagement and impact

1. Design and planning

First, I would like to ask you to imagine that you are a policy-maker yourself, and now ask yourself the following questions:
1. **Who am I?** This is important because this determines the target group of the policy brief. Are you targeting people within specific Government agencies, who are likely to have a relatively focused interest in the topic, with a relatively high degree of technical competence? In this case, you will need to include some of the technical detail, so that these specialists can make up their own mind about the credibility of your work. Or are you briefing policy analysts within Government departments who advise Ministers, or the MPs and Ministers themselves? In this case, your policy brief should be much shorter, with far less technical detail and much simpler language.
2. **When am I likely to read a policy brief?** This might determine when and how and in what format to distribute the brief (e.g. electronic, paper version, when to schedule the

email with the brief attached, such as an evening, even on weekends, will it be read over breakfast or on a train/flight?)

3. **How much time do I have to brief myself on research issues?** This is crucial for deciding the length of the 'brief'. If you are a high-ranking politician, you may only want to read a single page. Others might spend up to 30–60 minutes to get a more detailed picture of the research behind your recommendations. One approach is to do a 'breakfast test', as a policy brief should be read and understood in the length of time it takes to drink a coffee over breakfast.

4. **Why should I pick up the policy brief in the first place?** What is likely to grab your attention? How can you make it visually attractive, with a heading that is of interest? What sort of 'strapline' or 'teaser', perhaps based on a key finding, might encourage the politician to read it?

5. **What do I want to know?** What are the most pressing, wider policy issues? Can you link to important and current policy questions and issues? If your work is only one small contribution to a wider issue, can you collaborate with other researchers working in the same area to create a policy brief that includes your research, but that is likely to be perceived as having greater political significance? Is now the right time to put out your policy brief if there are other major issues swamping the policy agenda in your area?

6. **Is this compatible with my overarching goals and ideology as a policy-maker?** Many policy-makers are looking for research that furthers their own agenda and legitimises their views and ideology. They are unlikely to change these fundamental values and beliefs on the basis of one policy brief, so make sure you phrase your recommendations carefully, so that they do not instantly provoke a negative reaction based on a presumption of ideological incompatibility. This doesn't mean you need to make political recommendations or change your findings to fit the views of politicians — far from it. It is surprising, however, how far you can adapt the way in which you communicate your findings to make them attractive to different policy actors without altering the research in any way.

7. **Why has the researcher contacted me?** Do the targeted politicians have the power to actually change anything from the desired recommendations? Perhaps you should form a trusting relationship with them first to gain credibility.

8. **Who is this researcher anyway?** What indicators can quickly reassure a policy-maker with limited time that you are knowledgeable and credible enough to deliver the message? If you do not have a high profile yourself, what indicators of esteem might make them trust you by proxy, such as your institutional affiliation, the badge of your research funder or more senior academic mentors and supervisors who helped you write the brief?
9. **Are there clear and actionable things I can do as a result of reading this?** Is the evidence you provide aligned with the policy problem that the policy-maker needs to address? Can you provide solutions to these problems? Are your recommendations SMART (specific, measurable, achievable, relevant, and time-bound)? Can you make it even SMARTER (i.e. 'effective' e.g. cost-effective, and therefore more 'realistic')?

2. Writing and feedback loops

Now you have put yourself, effectively, in the shoes of your policy audience, you need to ask yourself:
- What would you like to get across yourself?
- What's your own aim for the policy brief?
- Does that match the policy-maker's perspective?

If your answer to the last question is "no", you should stop right there, otherwise you might be wasting your time.

If, however, you have been able to align your aims with the needs of policy-makers, it is now time to write the brief. With the help of the questions above, you will have already decided on length, style and language. You are using common terms without too much jargon, and avoiding (or if you have to, spelling out) acronyms. You are telling a convincing story about why change is needed.

How to set up the brief itself?

On the front page you'll need:
- **Title** — keep it short and powerful — would you personally pick up a policy brief with such a title? You can consider adding a subtitle, if it further explains your main message (again keep it short)

- **Teaser** — start with a summary of the brief's content and its relevance in two to three sentences, maximum five lines), state all the main points and repeat them throughout the document
- **Recommendations** — in bullet points, perhaps use a sidebar or box
- **Picture/photograph** — something attractive and positive that captures the research topic well. Make your picture bigger and have less text if possible

On the next pages, consider the following:
- **Overview** — give a brief overview and state the problem or objective. Embed your research in an important, current issue and explain how the policy brief contributes to that issue and provides useful answers.
- **Introduction** — summarise the issue, explain the context (including the political) to explain why the topic is so important and how your research can help to solve/improve the situation. Pinpoint gaps in current policy, link to crisis points that may be windows of opportunity in which new policies may be looked for. Outline a brief history or background, but only if it is relevant to the theme (otherwise leave it out!).
- **Research findings** — these are the answers from your research that help to solve the problem (other findings may be of interest to researchers and might look pretty on a graph, but if they don't help address the policy issue, cut them out). If possible, present your findings in a more visual, clear style, so the idea can be grasped immediately. Include research evidence from the literature and other sources to support your own findings in plain language. Use subheadings to break up blocks of text (keep sections of text and paragraphs as short as possible). Any graphs or other figures should be simple, and be labelled with a short description that can be understood without reading the text.
- **Sidebars and boxes** — highlight the most important evidence in sidebars or boxes, so people can easily skim through the key points if they are in a hurry (remember these are for highlighting important things, not for unimportant things, to policy-makers at least, like definitions)
- **White space and photographs** — try and break up your text with plenty of white space and photographs to avoid intimidating readers and also to make your work more

attractive to engage with. If you can, hire a professional designer to help with this. If there's not enough room to fit everything in that you want, don't make the font size smaller or cut white space and images — cut down your material (the next stage in the process, the feedback loop, will help with this if you're struggling to work out what you can cut)
- **Additional sources** — more (background) information, more detail on the topic, maximum four further sources, including peer-reviewed material by you and your team

Last page:
- Brief summary statement, concluding with the **take home message**
- **Policy recommendations** — clear recommendations aimed at specific policy sector(s) and specific live policy issues, in bullet points, stating why these options are recommended
- **Authors contact details** — including current position, associated institute and funder (remember the credibility issue), Twitter accounts (for key project staff and the project itself if this account exists), websites etc.
- **Acknowledgements**
- **Citations** — cite in footnotes, if needed

Revise and improve your brief: feedback loops

It is worth asking some creative people in your team to help with visual design, selection of photos, and also with wording. Give the brief to a non-academic friend. If he/she cannot understand your message, then you should consider rewriting. If you aim for EU policy-makers (most of which are non-English native speakers), try to give your draft to non-native English-speaking friends for feedback. Alternatively try the Up Goer Six website (http://www.splasho.com/upgoer6/), a text editor that colour codes all words according to how common they are. This will help you to identify jargon. Furthermore, if you want to get your message across, avoid being too directive e.g. telling policy-makers they "must" or "should" change policy. This can be tough, but psychologically this all makes a lot of sense. Are you happy being told what to do?

3. Distribution

How should you distribute your policy brief? The options are growing rapidly:

- **Electronically**: First you might upload your brand new policy brief to your own and your department/organisation's website. This will provide you with a link to a PDF of the brief that you can include in emails that you send out to your target group.

- **Hard copy**: Sending a 'paper' version to your target audience is important. Do not just send to a department, but make it personal and send it directly to a person. Even better, you can hand over your brief directly to policy-maker in a face-to-face meeting (be it over lunch, at a conference, during their 'office hours' — this might depend on your previous attempts to start a relationship with your target audience).

- **Social media and beyond**: Use the PDF link you created for all social media that you have set up personally and within your team, organisation, department or institution. That may (for example) include Twitter, ResearchGate, LinkedIn and even Facebook. Make sure to use a picture/photo of the cover (or key photo) of the brief to accompany distribution via social media as this attracts people and increases the likelihood of further distribution by sharing (liking, retweeting etc.) by others in your network. Make sure your profile on social media is consistent with your role as an expert in the field, with a link to your institution or a webpage that clearly links to it. The more times your target audience comes into contact with your material via different channels and people in their network, the more likely they are to perceive that it must be worth engaging with. For this reason you might also ask your PR department if they can publish a press release (together with the original research paper/research the brief is based on), on Twitter and so on. Furthermore, consider writing a blog post about the brief, that includes the recommendations, and distribute it through the channels mentioned above.

4. Engagement and impact

Follow up your email to your targeted people with a phone call. Ask if any further information is needed. Propose a lunchtime meeting or seminar to discuss your research further. Make sure the brief remains in the memory of your target group beyond the mere picking up and reading of the brief. You can also invite them to related conferences and workshops and take a copy of the brief with you to any of these events. Remember that one-way information flows are unlikely to get anyone to act on your recommendations.

If you are not likely to meet the target of your policy brief any time soon in person, you might start following them via Twitter (as mentioned earlier, lots of policy-makers are active on this platform nowadays) or subscribe to email lists to know what they are up to and to learn where your work fits in and contributes towards their agenda. Take the time to find out what they think, what sort of language they use, what is on their agenda and see what they believe can help them with their daily tasks. And once you have the chance to meet them in person, your connection via social media will make it easier to build trust. As Onora O'Neill said so beautifully in her TED talk about how to trust intelligently:

"If you make yourself vulnerable to the other party, then that is very good evidence that you are trustworthy."

Active listening works wonders too.

Perhaps you will find forming trusting relationships so fruitful that you decide to co-produce the policy briefs in collaboration with the people who will use it. This is a particularly effective way to develop the policy brief according to their needs and will ensure that it is used and result in impact.

To be able to achieve impact, the best-case scenario is that you already have a long-lasting trusting relationship with relevant policy-makers. But it is not too late; you can start now. Find out the events they are likely to attend, and look up photographs of them, so that you can identify them during breaks to introduce yourself to them and get to know them. Policy-makers are just people like us. If you find it difficult to start small talk by yourself, ask colleagues to help. They may already be trusted by the policy-maker and may be able to introduce you to them. Some of this trust will make your initial contact more trustworthy too.

Examples

Finally, I'd like to show you a few examples of policy briefs that I think are particularly good. The first was developed by Julia McMorrow from the University of Manchester, and is notable because it led to concrete changes in Government policy. It raised cross-sector awareness of wildfire and helped make the case for severe wildfire to be included for the first time on the National Risk Register in 2013. The Chair of the Chief Fire Officers Wildfire Group commented:

"Such was the quality of the Policy Brief, that I used it to raise the awareness of wildfire issues affecting UK Fire and Rescue Services by circulating it to all Chief Fire Officers... The work is as relevant now as it was when first produced in 2010. The FIRES Policy Brief also formed a cornerstone of the Wildfire Group's initial Action Plan."

The policy brief recommended better fire reporting and as a result, Julia was invited to work with the Fire Service to evaluate how satellite data and their Incident Recording System could be used to understand national and regional wildfire distribution. The joint research developed criteria to differentiate 'wildfires' from other less significant vegetation fires and recommended ways to improve reporting. The definition was used in the Scottish Government's Wildfire Operational Guidance. The work has also been used as an example to influence wildfire policy in Ireland. Julia was invited to join the England and Wales Wildfire Forum, the Fire and Statistics User Group and other national and regional stakeholder groups.

I asked Julia what she thought had made it such an effective policy brief, and she explained the long path that she and her colleagues took to develop it. First, she organised a series of seminars, to which she invited all the key stakeholders who were affected by the issues she and others were researching. Part of this was about presenting and discussing her research findings, but it was also about understanding how different stakeholders perceived the research, and understanding their knowledge of the issues too. She ensured that the steering group of the seminar series was composed equally of practitioners and researchers. They jointly took the policy brief forward, deciding on the language to be used, and the framing of the key messages, ensuring all the time that it remained based firmly on the seminars' findings. Part of the group was an organisation who already ran a successful series of briefing notes on related topics, so their design template was used to reach their existing audience and make it as widely accessible as possible. Julia explained:

"The most rewarding part of developing this policy brief was the relationships we built leading up to and during the process, which have stood the test of time. It also opened doors to influential national stakeholder groups. In both these ways, it continues to bring us new opportunities to realise impacts from our research."

For me, this is a really powerful example of the relational approach to developing policy briefs I've described in this chapter. The priority of the team was on building long-term, two-way, trusting relationships through a series of meetings, which enabled them to co-produce the text. Whatever design ideas the team might have had were put aside, so that an existing, well-recognised design template could be used. This enabled the team to make the material as widely available as possible. After the policy brief was published, the research team were able to continue working closely with the members of the practitioner and policy community who had been involved in the seminar series to effect policy change.

Finding attractively designed policy briefs is remarkably hard. However, the National Institute for Early Education Research (NIEER) have a highly visual format to their policy brief series, which I love (Figure 14). Their briefs are full-colour throughout with page colours selected to match colours in the photographs that feature on each page. As you can see from the front page below, policy recommendations are clearly identified and highlighted here, along with a summary of the literature on the topic (not just the narrow findings of one particular study). The Evidence Matters series is similarly colourful, featuring full-colour photographs on the front page (Figure 14). This series operates like a magazine, with monthly briefings on a specific issue. Having regular releases of new policy briefs helps raise the profile of a series, keeping copies regularly at the top of the pile on coffee tables in the offices of those you want to reach out to. The CLAHRC bites series is also colourful, featuring eye-catching and often emotionally powerful images (Figure 15). It is a great example of what can be done with a short format. These bite-sized summaries of evidence are only two sides of A5 paper, but they convey the evidence concisely and powerfully.

Figure 14: Examples of policy briefs from the Evidence Matters and NIEER series

The University of **Nottingham**
UNITED KINGDOM · CHINA · MALAYSIA

CLAHRC **BITE**

A bite-sized summary of a piece of **CLAHRC** research

January 2013
BITE 20

Who this applies to:

Practitioners prescribing for patients with moderate-to-severe Alzheimer's disease.

Findings and implications...

- Cholinesterase inhibitors were effective for severe Alzheimer's disease .

- These findings are inconsistent with the literature on which NICE guidance was based (due to be updated in 2014) which recommends AChE inhibitors, such as donepezil, for mild to moderate Alzheimer's disease and memantine for severe disease.

- This study recommends treatment with cholinesterase inhibitor should be considered in the awareness of the increased risks of adverse outcomes including syncope, the need for permanent pacemakers and hip fractures.

While donepezil is currently recommended for patients with mild or moderate Alzheimer's, recent data indicates that donepezil gives cognitive and functional benefits for patients with moderate or severe disease.

The Bigger Picture

This multicentre study in England and Scotland (Howard, R. et al 2012) investigated the effectiveness of donepezil and memantine as patients' disease progressed. Patients who had moderate or severe Alzheimer's disease and were living in the community were recruited for the trial.

Participants were randomised to one of four groups; continuing on donepezil; discontinuing donepezil; memantine with donepezil; or memantine while donepezil was discontinued.

Patients in the group assigned to continue receiving donepezil showed significant benefit compared to the group who discontinued donepezil. The SMMSE indicated that on average cognitive function was better for the donepezil group (1.9 points, 95% confidence interval (CI) 1.3 to 2.5). The BADLS measure indicated lower impairment for the donepezil group (3.0 points (95% CI, 1.8 to 4.3) (P<0.001 for both comparisons).

Treatment with memantine in addition to donepezil did not yield significant differences.

Patients assigned to receive memantine showed significantly better outcomes in comparison to the group assigned to receive memantine placebo. Both primary outcomes show improvements; SMMSE was an average of 1.2 points higher (95% CI, 0.6 to 1.8; P<0.001) and BADLS was 1.5 points lower (95% CI, 0.3 to 2.8; P=0.02).

For the donepezil group, the average outcome differences were larger than the clinically important differences for the cognitive function measure (SMMSE, 1.4), however the difference in the measure of impairment was lower than the clinical important level (BADLS, 3.5). For the memantine group, while significant changes were observed in both cognitive function and impairment, neither of these reached a level of clinical importance.

The Evidence

Gill, S. S., et al 2009 "Syncope and its consequences in patients with dementia receiving cholinesterase inhibitors: a population-based cohort study" Archives of internal medicine 169(9): 867

Howard, R., et al 2012 "Donepezil and memantine for moderate-to severe Alzheimer's disease." New England journal of medicine 366(10): 893-903

Kaduszkiewicz, H., et al 2005 "Cholinesterase inhibitors for patients with Alzheimer's disease: systematic review of randomised clinical trials." Bmj 331(7512): 321-27.

National Institute for Health and Clinical Excellence. 2011. "Donepezil, galantamine, rivastigmine and memantine for the treatment of Alzheimer's disease. NICE technology appraisal guidance 217."

An explanation of CLAHRC and its role

The Collaboration for Leadership in Applied Health Research and Care (CLAHRC) is a partnership between the University of Nottingham and the NHS in Nottinghamshire, Derbyshire and Lincolnshire.

Funded by the National Institute for Health Research, our mission is to undertake high quality research to improve health and social care across the East Midlands.

This is a bite-sized summary of a piece of CLAHRC research. It is part of a series designed to make such work more available to clinicians.

Our website
www.clahrc-ndl.nihr.ac.uk

Useful link
www.alzheimers.org.uk

Contact us
tom.dening@nottingham.ac.uk

This is a summary of independent research funded by Medical Research Council and Alzheimer's Society

The views expressed are those of the author(s) and not necessarily those of the NHS, the NIHR or the Department of Health.

Figure 15: Example of a CLAHRC bite

Figure 16: Example policy brief from the Living With Environmental Change policy brief series (pages 1–4, clockwise from top right)

In contrast to these, the Living With Environmental Change policy briefs are monochrome green, but this was done for a clear purpose (Figure 16). Anne Liddon, the series editor, explained to me:

"We launched a similar series ten years ago with the research councils' Rural Economy Land Use programme (RELU) which had a slightly different focus. The RELU policy briefs were incredibly successful and we gained a reputation for providing timely and relevant research findings to Government and other stakeholders. We worked hard on the RELU brand, and the policy briefs were instantly recognisable as part of the programme. So when RELU ended and Living With Environmental Change wanted to launch a new series, we managed to merge the branding so the new series kept the same look and format. This meant policy-makers instantly recognised and trusted the new series as a reputable source of information that could inform their decisions."

One of the things that is interesting about this is the importance of brand reputation and recognition for policy briefs. You can just create your own design template and do your own thing. However, if you can find an existing policy brief series that has already built a relevant audience and has a strong reputation, your policy recommendations are more likely to be read and paid attention. If you are starting a new policy brief series, work on your brand and create something distinctive, attractive and instantly recognisable.

The Living With Environmental Change series is a great example of what a good policy brief can look like, particularly on the inside pages. As series editor, Anne encouraged researchers to focus on specific key findings, rather than covering the whole research project, with a strong emphasis on the implications for policy. The front page has an image that tries to capture the content of the brief. In this example, it took a long time to find an image for air quality. The researcher wanted a positive image of air quality, so pictures of traffic and exhaust pipes were out. However, the researcher's suggestion of a landscape image did not seem obvious enough. Eventually Anne sourced an image of a colleague's daughter running with a kite, and the search was over. On the inner pages, there is always plenty of white (or green) space around the text, no matter how much the researcher pleads to add more words. The introductory paragraph lays out the problem being addressed, and each heading is a question that Anne thinks the audience will want to ask. Finally, there is a box section with concrete action points for the audience and further information.

There are many more examples I could show you, but these four give you a flavour of the sort of thing that is possible. I've chosen them because they provide important lessons that illustrate and complement the suggestions I've made earlier in the chapter. However, take a look around for yourself at policy briefs, whether or not they are linked to your research area, and draw on the best ideas.

Chapter 21
How to evidence and write up your impact

If your research has had beneficial impacts in the real world, then there's a good chance you'll want (or have) to shout about it. In this chapter, I will distil the best advice that is currently available about how to collect evidence to demonstrate your impact and write this up as a case study.

Evidencing your impact

There are many ways you can evidence research impacts, and these vary from discipline to discipline. In Arts and Humanities disciplines, for example, evidence of public engagement (e.g. via media coverage and visitor numbers) is more important than for many science disciplines.

Instrumental impacts tend to be easier to characterise clearly and evidence than other types of impact, such as conceptual or capacity-building impacts (see Box 1 for an overview of different types of impact). Where you have evidence of instrumental impacts, it is still worth looking for evidence of other types of impact, even if these were part of the 'pathway' to your instrumental impact. A good case study shows the pathway to impact as clearly as the impact itself, and can make the communication of impact more powerful. In cases where there is no evidence of instrumental impacts, it is particularly important to evidence the significance of the impact, or create a compelling argument to demonstrate that instrumental impacts are inevitable as a result of the types of impact that have already been realised.

Bear in mind that the impact of your research is likely to be evaluated alongside impacts from other researchers working in similar areas, and the types and standards of evidence that are deemed suitable to claim impact vary across disciplines. For example, in medicine, randomised controlled trials are the gold standard to evidence the impact of an intervention. Where policy impacts are concerned, it is widely accepted that there are huge challenges associated with time lags and attribution, and so it is more common to see evidence in the form of references to research in policy documents supported by narrative statements from members of the policy community. Quantification of impacts numerically can be useful to demonstrate tangible, measurable benefits, but for many impacts, qualitative evidence is more appropriate (and may be the only type of data available).

Very often, researchers look for evidence of impact after the research has been done and impacts are expected to have occurred. This can be problematic for a number of reasons. First, there are many types of evidence that are impossible to derive after impacts have occurred, and if impact monitoring is not built into the research project, important opportunities for collecting data may be missed. For example, a simple head count of visitors to an exhibition may help demonstrate the impact of work, but if this data is not collected during the exhibition, it is very difficult to credibly estimate this later. The second problem is that if you don't monitor progress towards your impact goals, there is no way of knowing when you are failing to make progress or taking backwards steps. If you are tracking the effects of each activity you carry out on your planned pathway to impact, you will quickly find out if these activities are not working, or leading to unintended consequences. However, if you do not ask yourself, your team or your stakeholders how these activities are going, then you may only find out that things were going horribly wrong long after there is any opportunity to correct your course.

It is for these reasons, that I suggest identifying impact indicators linked to your goals and activities at the outset, when you are first planning for impact (Chapters 3 and 9). The impact planning template in Section 4 includes a column for you to identify these indicators, and it suggests that you also identify ways of measuring each indicator. The reason I have suggested doing this is that it is often easy to come up with indicators that are very difficult to measure, despite clearly telling you whether an activity has worked and tracking progress towards an impact goal. If an indicator is going to be difficult to measure, then you either need to budget for the resources necessary to measure it, or you need to come up with an indicator that will be easier or more cost-effective to measure.

There are a number of ways of coming up with impact indicators. Some will be self-evident, such as the value of a spin-out company or the number of lives saved by a new safety technology. However, even apparently self-evident indicators may be difficult to collect data on, for example, if the company is not willing to disclose profits or your relationship is with the company who make the technology rather than those who use it. These examples show how the process of identifying indicators can actually feed back into your impact planning, as you realise that you will need to initiate new relationships or strengthen trust with key individuals.

Where indicators are not obvious, it may be necessary to use your imagination to come up with examples of the sorts of things you might expect to change or happen if you achieved your impact. For example, if you wanted to change perceptions of Asian cinema in Europe, you might expect to see changes in the categories in film awards and the composition of judges on film award panels. Eventually this might translate into an increase in the number of Asian films shown on television and in cinemas, with increased viewing numbers. However, if viewing figures were your only indicator of impact, you might miss important changes that demonstrate the influence of your research. In this particular case, the person researching Asian film hadn't been looking at awards, and didn't have a plan of activities to get her research into the awards community. Again, this is a good example of indicator identification pointing to missing activities that can measurably increase impact.

So what makes a good impact indicator? During my PhD, I reviewed the literature on indicators, and found that there are a number of characteristics you might want to look for in a good indicator. Depending on the timescales you are working with, and your budget, some of these characteristics may be more important to you than others.

What makes a good indicator of research impact?

A good indicator of research impact should be:
- **Accurate and bias free:** a good indicator should actually tell you about the impact of your research (or the impact of the activity you designed to deliver impact from your research), rather than just describing the pathway to impact. For example, rather than just measuring the number of people who attend your events, give them a questionnaire to ask how your event changed their perceptions and what they will do differently as a result, and try and get their contact details and permission to follow them up later to see if they put what they learned into practice

- **Relevant, reliable and consistent in a range of different circumstances:** you don't want to choose indicators that will only give you accurate information in one country or culture if you expect your impact to occur across multiple countries and cultures. Similarly, one measure might work for one public audience or stakeholder group, but not apply to another
- **Timely:** it is useful if your indicators can provide you with information in a timely manner, for example, within a reporting window for your funder. Also, if it takes too long to collect or analyse the data you need, you may find out that something isn't working too late, and be unable to correct your course
- **Robust and credible:** consider your indicators from the perspective of the people who will be learning about your impacts, and assess whether or not you think that the evidence you are collecting is likely to be perceived as being robust and credible. You may have designed evidence collection in a way that you know is highly credible, but the simple fact that you are collecting that data as the researcher who is claiming the impact may undermine the credibility of your evidence. Consider if there is some way to get the evidence you need collected and published by an independent, credible third party. Check whether the indicators you have chosen have been used by others and whether they are respected or not. For example, the case study later in this chapter, "Discover Turner's Yorkshire", used 'Advertising Value Equivalency' to estimate the value of media coverage. This measures column inches devoted to stories about your research and then looks at the price that the publication charges for advertising space, and uses this to convert the column inches into a financial value. However, this approach makes many assumptions (e.g. that the whole article is actually about your research, and that the coverage is positive) and as a result is discouraged by the Chartered Institute for Public Relations (CIPR). CIPR offer guidance on alternative, more robust measures, such as qualitative research via interviews and focus groups, and quantitative research via polls, surveys and other studies that can credibly measure the impact of your work
- **Independently verifiable and replicable:** good indicators have an evidence trail behind them that can be traced by anyone who wants to understand how you arrived at the

numbers you have claimed in relation to your impact. As I mentioned in the previous point, having evidence published by an independent third party helps make your evidence credible. However, this is even better if there is a transparent method that has been used to collect the data which could be replicated if someone wanted to check the figures for themselves

- **Linked to clear targets or baselines:** it is sometimes difficult to interpret the importance of a change in an indicator if you are unable to see the original baseline level from which it has changed, or how far it has changed towards an impact target. You should already have SMART impact objectives that you're planning for and monitoring progress towards, so make sure that you've found as many indicators as possible that could enable you to see if you are moving towards or away from these objectives. In addition to this, it can be useful to consider your baseline. Very often, to determine the baseline from which your research is building impact, you will need to assess this at the start of your project. For example, if you expect a habitat to be saved or restored as a result of your research, then you will need to know how much of the habitat there is when you started your work, and what condition that remaining habitat is in. This illustrates the importance of identifying indicators while you are planning for impact at the outset.

If you're struggling to come up with measurable indicators, here are some examples of impact evidence you can explore:

- Google key statistics or phrases from your work to see where they have been used in documents that have been put on the web
- Did people pay for advice or did consultancy work arise from the research, and can you track the flows of money?
- What is the readership of a particular newspaper or online media source and how might this translate into money via advertising revenues linked to page views and circulation? Retain date-stamped copies of the web pages in case the web links change
- In public engagement case studies, can you show evidence of your research being widely disseminated and talked about or used? Did you blog your research and how many people read the blogs? Did you tweet it? Did you get any press or broadcast coverage? Did any trade journals or close-to-policy

journals or websites cover the work? What is the diversity of the audiences reached?

- Did particular target groups attend project events? This could involve retaining delegate lists from conferences or workshops (particularly if policy-makers and media attended) and following these up to assess if there was any benefit or change as a result
- Is there any evidence of sales, downloads or access to web content, and how did this increase over time?
- Did you get letters of support from external bodies before you submitted the grant that funded your research? If so, can you go back to these organisations to see how they used your work? Who did they pass your work onto or talk to about your research, and at what decision-making level? Can these people point you to evidence in documents etc. that your work has been used? If not, can they provide testimonials about the impact of your work?
- Did your engagement with stakeholder continue after the project? If so, what further collaborations arose from this engagement that wouldn't have happened without the original research? Did collaborators use the methods from the research in their own professional practice after the research ended, and what was the effect of those changes in their practice?

Finally, consider different ways in which you can communicate your case study to the world. The marketing department of the organisation you work for will probably be interested in featuring your impact in their work. You may be able to interest a journalist in co-authoring a feature article for a Sunday newspaper or magazine, based on the impact of your research. The more widely you can disseminate your success, the more likely others will find your research and want to work with you to develop new impacts.

Key points for writing an effective impact case study

1. Create a coherent narrative that explains clearly the relationship between the underpinning research and the impact.
It may be useful to briefly explain what was original or distinctive about the research that contributed to the impacts. Consider starting from the perspective of the beneficiaries — how did they benefit and why is that benefit so important to them? Be as specific as possible if you want the link between the research and the impact to be credible,

including specific details about the names of researchers, their positions and dates and locations of the research activity. Choose a strong headline for your case study and ensure your summary starts with a powerful opening sentence that summarises the case study and draws the reader in.

2. **Be as clear as possible about exactly what the impact was,** adding some sort of precise quantification with numbers wherever possible. Quantitative data and indicators need to be meaningful and contextualised to clearly support the case being made, not used as a substitute for a clear narrative. Avoid generalised or exaggerated statements about your impact.

3. **Clearly identify specifically who has benefited from the work** or which groups/organisations have changed something as a result of the research. Bear in mind that this may include 'intermediary' organisations as well as your intended 'end users' or audiences.

4. **Be concise.** A concise case study that pulls out the key points easily for readers has far greater impact than one that is dense and rambling. If you've not been given one already, you could consider imposing some sort of page or word constraint on your case studies.

5. **Keep your language simple and direct.** If possible, get advice from a science writer or communications specialist, but try and avoid introducing inaccuracies. Remember your audience, and that your audience is probably not other academics. Readers should not have to have in-depth expert or prior knowledge to be able to understand your case study. It is essential that impact case studies avoid academic jargon, so that they are accessible to all your readers. If possible, divide your text up with headings and bullets or bold text that clearly signposts your key impacts to readers, so they don't have to search through large bodies of text for the key points.

6. If you are writing multiple case studies, **identify key features of best practice and be consistent** about all your case studies covering these aspects. You might, for example, want to consider a particular list of subheadings for each case study to follow. However, avoid making all your case studies sound too similar; even if they are written by the same person, if you want them to also feel authentic.

7. Related to this, make sure you **provide detailed, specific and independent evidence** to support every claim you make. All material required for readers to judge your impact needs to be

contained within the case study. Avoid anecdotal evidence or evidence that might perceived as such. If possible, link to published evidence that demonstrates the impact of your research. It is possible to commission work to demonstrate impacts yourself, but you will need to consider carefully how this will be published, to ensure that it is perceived to be sufficiently independent and credible. Rather than just listing sources of evidence, explain how each source of evidence supports a specific aspect of the impact that has been claimed.

8. Bring your case studies to life with **quotes that illustrate the impact** with greater resonance than could otherwise be done with formal language. If these quotes are from people with high-profile and relevant job titles, then this adds significant credibility to your case study, as well as some lived experience. Finding quotes from people years after an impact has occurred can be tricky, however, so it is recommended to collect these from people as the impact unfolds, and if nothing else, keep track of contact details so that people can be easily contacted later. Bear in mind that key people who could attest to the impact of your work may retire or die before you need to write your case study. Usually it is best to aim for a good balance of quantitative data and quotes to support impacts. However, in case studies where there is no quantitative data to corroborate an impact (e.g. a policy which has been developed but not yet implemented), quotes may be the primary source of corroboration to evidence your impact.

Creating an impact case study is partly about having high quality evidence to corroborate your claims. However, it is partly about the narrative you create, as the following examples illustrate. Organising your evidence into a coherent narrative that shows the pathway to your current impact and your trajectory towards future impacts can make the difference between a case study that reads as a list or one that reads as a transformative journey.

For example, in the 2014 assessment of research impact under the UK Government's Research Excellence Framework, my peatland research (illustrated in the impact planning template worked example in Section 4) was considered to have "very considerable impacts in terms of their reach and significance" (and awarded three out of four stars). This judgment was made despite the fact that, at the time of submitting my case study, the research had not yet led to a change in Government policy and that policy had not been implemented to achieve change on the ground. However, there was a clear enough impact on various policy processes that an impact on policy and on the ground appeared inevitable (and these impacts are now actually happening as predicted). It probably also helped that many of the other impacts in my field were related to policy, and the difficulties of demonstrating this type of impact are well known to assessors.

Similarly, there is a perception that arts and humanities case studies that have "reach and significance" need to go beyond raising public awareness and demonstrating engagement with the research, to actually achieving instrumental impacts as well. Although this might enhance a case study if such impacts have occurred, there are many examples of very convincing (and top-scoring) impact case studies from the arts and humanities that demonstrated their impacts purely in terms of engagement and reach. The final section of this chapter will review a few examples of impact case studies drawn from UK research, however, the generalisable lessons from these case studies is applicable wherever you are doing research in the world.

Examples

'Turner's Yorkshire' is an example of impact arising from research in fine art. Professor David Hill from the University of Leeds published extensively on Turner's work, highlighting Yorkshire as a landscape of international significance. His fieldwork tracked the artist's travels through the county, locating, examining and photographing his viewpoints as they survive today. A tourist promotion, "Discover

Turner's Yorkshire", gave this work much wider public impact, with published and online materials, such as the Turner's Trails website (with walking routes and audio guides), raising public awareness of the significance of the county to the artist (Figure 17). This increased tourism and brought economic and social benefits, which the researchers quantified as far as possible in their case study.

What interests me about this as an example of an impact case study, is the comprehensive and innovative use of evidence:
- 100,000 page views, 10,000 downloads
- Estimated 1.25 million visitors seen interpretation boards
- Visitors to Turner Trails spent on average £199 per head per trip
- Over 50% of local tourism businesses thought the project had a positive effect on business
- Extensive media coverage equating to £600,000 in total Advertising Value Equivalency (note: this measure is not viewed as being credible nowadays)

Figure 17: Screenshot from Turner Trails website

Cardiff University's DECIPHer-Assist project claims to be the UK's most effective school-based smoking prevention programme. Peer-nominated students aged 12–13 were taught how to intervene as 'peer supporters' with their Year 8 peers in everyday situations to discourage them from smoking. The impact of this education research was given the highest possible grade in the UK's Research Excellence Framework. Evidence of the impact included:

- Over 60,000 students have taken part since 2010
- Cited as good practice in policy documents
- Cardiff research suggests 1,650 young people will not go on to take up smoking as a result
- Treatment of lung cancer in England costs £261M per year. If implemented throughout the UK, ASSIST would prevent 20,000 young people taking up smoking each year
- Award-winning company set up to licence the programme

A University of York sociology project called "Advising the advisers" helped improve the conduct of adviser-claimant interviews in Jobcentres. This impact was also awarded the highest possible grade for its significance and reach. Policy-makers learned about evidence via working papers and presentations, and changes in policy resulted from the work, including new procedures & compulsory training for advisors. This impact was evidence, using testimonials from those who had benefited from the work, such as this one, from a senior civil servant:

"This research has had impacts in immediate and potentially long term performance gains. We are now using the results of this research to develop and test [an evidence-based] adviser training programme. The results of this research have the potential to change the whole adviser training approach"

These examples show the wide range of different types of impacts and evidence that can be used in case studies. They also show how differently impact is evidenced in different disciplines. You can read thousands more in detail at impact.hefce.ac.uk. It is worth dipping into this database. Browse through case studies in your subject area or search for keywords you are working on if you want some inspiration. Read through the descriptions of impact to get new ideas about types of evidence you could collect and use to communicate your own impacts.

Chapter 22
Conclusion: left hanging (with the right tools for the job)

One of the most powerful metaphors for my approach to impact is this image of a man who has been lowered over the edge of a roof to fix a sign (Figure 18). You have to assume that these two men know and trust each other, given the level of trust that the dangling man has clearly placed in his colleague. One can imagine the conversation that preceded this operation, as they discussed what might be wrong with the sign, and who would volunteer to be lowered into position.

Figure 18: Two men fixing a sign on a Russian furniture store

For me, this explains the heart of this book: impact is based on long-term, trusting, equal relationships, and two-way communication between researchers and those interested in our work. As we work together, we negotiate our goals and carefully plan together how we will reach them, considering the roles we will each play in the process.

Only in this context does it become relevant to ask if we've got the right tool for the job. In the case of the two workmen, we can assume that the man dangling over the roof knew that he would need a screwdriver. We might also assume that if he's holding a flat-headed screwdriver in his hand, he might have a different type of screwdriver in his pocket, just in case. When we're planning for impact we need the right tools for the job, and it is always good to have a Plan B, in case the activity we planned doesn't deliver the desired results.

I want to make an important point of emphasis with this metaphor. It is easy to skip to this third section of the book and pick and choose tools and techniques to achieve impact. But if we do this, there is a real danger that we miss the whole point of impact, which is to create social and economic benefits that make the world a better place. Impact then becomes a box-ticking exercise in which stakeholders and members of the public are left feeling used and bemused by their interactions with us. There are plenty of toolboxes available that will inspire you to try all manner of exciting new knowledge exchange activities. But if our focus is on the toolbox rather than the context in which to use those tools, then we may be tempted to drop the people we are working with, when the project ends. Like the man holding his colleague for as long as it takes, holding onto relationships for the long term can sometimes be hard work. But if you invest in relationships over the long term, you'll be around when the opportunity arises for your research to be put into action. And the people and organisations you're working with will be around when you need a letter of support for your next grant application.

Research impact is a collaborative endeavour – we can't do it on our own. So let's swallow our pride and adopt an attitude of service that identifies and responds to opportunities as they arise. If researchers start co-producing knowledge with the people who need it most, the ideas we come up with really will change the world. None of us has to do anything particularly big, but taken together, we have enough collective intelligence to solve almost any problem, if we will just work together.

You don't have to be a natural communicator or extrovert. You don't even need to be that confident. Your research can make an impact, even if you are chronically shy, if you have the heart for it, a plan and a few relevant skills. My 'eureka' moment came at a time in my life when I was facing the causes of my own chronic lack of confidence. Having experienced sexual abuse throughout my childhood, I had very little sense of 'self', let alone self-confidence. As an academic I lived in constant fear of what others thought of me. Each professional failure appeared to confirm the sense of self-loathing that was always lurking beneath the surface, no matter how bright and cheerful a face I put on. I found engaging with stakeholders terrifying for years. I would sit outside people's offices with sweaty palms and heart thumping, feeling sick before entering each meeting. The fear only became greater with time, as the people became more important and the stakes higher. But I pushed through that fear, believing that through my actions, I could give many times more to the world, than that one person had taken from me, as I grew up.

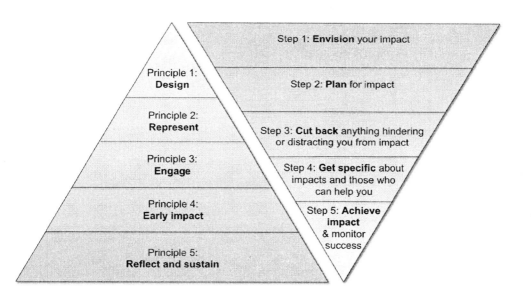

All of us have something we can give back to the world, no matter how small and insignificant we might feel our research is. No matter how much fear the steps in this book might hold for you, it is possible to push through your fear and take those steps towards impact. You don't need to change who you are, or try and become like anyone else. You can take these steps, whether you are a scientist or an arts and humanities scholar; a PhD student or a professor; confident or terrified. Unfortunately for me, being me has meant embracing the fear. However, it turns out that "just being me" makes people more likely to take my research seriously and engage with me. That's one of the reasons that I wanted to write this handbook very much "as me" rather than as a dry, third-person account of how to generate impact from research. I can't put myself in the shoes of everyone reading this book, but it is my hope that you now have itchy feet and are ready to put yourself in the shoes of those who might use your research. If you feel overwhelmed by the amount of information in this handbook, all you have to do is connect with the people who are interested in your research and the rest will come naturally.

The steps in this book, underpinned by each of the five principles, have the power to enable all of us to start generating and sharing knowledge in new ways. As we work more closely with those who are interested in our work, or who want to use it, we will learn how to generate knowledge that is more interesting and useful, and can effect change in ways we would never have imagined possible. Even if each of us only makes a small change through our research, if we can be that change, together we have the potential to change the world. To me, this book is a bit like a dandelion. To some it will be an inspirational wildflower, while to others it will be a weed for the compost heap. But for me it is a wish, as I blow its seeds into the wind and hope that a few of them take root in your research. It is impossible to predict which way the wind will blow these seeds, but that's what makes sharing ideas so exciting.

Part 4: Templates and examples

Stakeholder Analysis Template

Name of individual, group or organisation	Likely interest in your research H/M/L	What aspects of your research are they likely to be interested in? Identify key messages linked directly to your research for this group	What level of influence (positive or negative) might they have on your ability to complete the research and generate impacts? H/M/L	Comments on influence (e.g. times or contexts in which they have more/less influence over the outcomes of your research, ways they might block or facilitate your research or impact)	If influence is high but interest is low, how might we motivate greater interest and engagement with the research?	Any important relationships with other stakeholders? (e.g. conflicts/ alliances)	Any modes of communicatio n preferred or that should be avoided?

Worked example

This is based on a hypothetical stakeholder analysis developed for a project funded by the Swedish International Development and Cooperation Agency (Sida), led by the Regional Environment Centre in cooperation with local partner IUCN ROWA. The Water SUM project (http://www.watersum.rec.org/), for which this was developed, is using this template to train country teams how to conduct a stakeholder analysis in preparation for local water security action planning in collaboration with stakeholders. Column headings have been adapted for the purpose of this project. As long as you capture the level and nature of interest and influence in some way, you can add and remove columns from the matrix as necessary. However, remember that the more columns you add, the more time-consuming it will be to complete.

Name of organisation/ group	Interest H/M/L	What are current levels of involvement in water management planning, and what aspects of local water security action planning (LWSAP) are they (likely to be) most interested in?	If involvement and/or interest is L/M, how might we motivate engagement with LWSAP? What benefits might they derive from being more involved in LWSAP?	Level of knowledge about water related issues H/M/L	Access to high quality information about water-related issues H/M/L	Influence on water management H/M/L	Comments on influence (e.g. attitudes to water management planning, times or contexts in which they have more/less influence)	Any important relationships with other stakeholders? (e.g. conflicts/alliances)
Households	H	Involvement in water management planning varies significantly between households, but all households are water users, and significantly affected by water management	N/A	L	L	L	None	Many households in the area rely on agriculture for at least part of their income, hence strong links with both types of farming

248

Stakeholder		Description					stakeholder below
Farmers using irrigated land	H	Farmers with land close to water sources growing crops that depend on irrigation water are heavy water users and significantly affected by water quality and quantity issues	N/A	M	L	M	Those within the farming union and co-operatives have a more organised, stronger voice	Strong relationships with wider farming community including upland rain-fed farmers
Rain-fed upland farmers	L	Interested indirectly as householders or where they also own irrigated lowland fields, but otherwise not directly affected by changes in water flow or quality	Given low interest and influence, it is not a priority to engage with this group	L	L	L	None	Strong relationships with irrigated farming community, often through family ties
Farmer's Union	H	The Farmer's Union has been putting pressure on Government for some time not to restrict access to irrigated water, and to invest in schemes to pipe water from other regions to this area	N/A	H	M	M	Despite having strong relationships with some politicians, the Farmer's Union has failed to achieve the objectives it has been campaigning for	Irrigated farmers are well represented in the Union, but upland farmers feel under-represented and membership from this group is much lower
Local small businesses that depend on regular flows of clean water e.g. food and	H	Without adequate alternative supplies, problems with water quality and quantity are a major problem for some businesses in the area	N/A	L	L	L	None	Few small business have strong links with the Government, farming or NGO communities, which reduces their influence

drink sector								
Multinational businesses	L	The local steel works is water-intensive, but is located upstream from most other water users, and so has preferential access to low flows, and has little interest in the problems this creates downstream, especially during drought years	Explore how more efficient water use might reduce costs and hence increase profits for the company. Look for evidence of failures to meet regulatory requirements to see if legal action could be taken. Explore potential for public campaign (including via print and social media) to exert pressure on the company	L	H	H	Water use by this company is one of the key causes of low flows, and increased pollution levels	The CEO has married into a wealthy local family who have farming interests
Government public health agencies	M	High interest in specific areas where pollution is leading to health problems and during drought years, but otherwise less directly interested in water management	N/A	L	M	L	There is a lack of communication between different Government departments and agencies	Generally disconnected from other stakeholders affected by these issues
Environmental protection agencies from Government	H	Statutory obligation to monitor and manage water resources	N/A	H	H	M	Due to limited resources, this agency has historically not been able to effect significant change in water resources	There is conflict between these agencies and environmental NGOs who have been putting pressure on them

						management	to improve water management
IUCN water management project	H	High interest within the project team that is focusing on water management	N/A	H	H	M	At this point, the project is not well enough known to be able to estimate its influence, but if the project achieves its goals, then it will have been highly influential. Of course, if it does not achieve its goals, then its influence will have been low	Strong relationships with eNGOs and Government (one of the only environmental organisations to have positive relationships with the environmental protection agency)
Other environmental NGOs	M	Other eNGOs are focusing on a wide range of topics, and do not have specific programmes relating to water management, however, they are indirectly interested when problems with water management compromise species and habitats that they are working on	N/A	M	M	L	Don't tend to work specifically on water management, so have relatively little influence over water management issues	Involved in a number of long-standing conflicts over nature conservation and natural resource management with the Government
Local University	H	There is a strong research group focusing on Integrated Water Management who are collaborating with the IUCN project	N/A	H	H	L	The group has not been engaged with stakeholders much in the past	Although links with other stakeholders are weak, the group is widely trusted by others

Example event facilitation plan

Stakeholder mapping workshop for AFRP Innovation Forum

Aim: to identify organisations and groups with a stake in the future of sustainable food production in the UK, which may be interested in co-producing knowledge with researchers from AFRP

09.45   Tea/coffee

10.00 Introduction and scoping
- Introductions
- Clarify the scope of the forum by geographical scale, sector etc. (where should our focus lie?)

10.20 Introduction to stakeholder analysis
- Introduction to stakeholder analysis and example using blank matrix on wall. Key points: defining interest and influence (both positive and negative), checking for redundant or missing columns
- Explain columns:
  - Name of organisation or group
  - Interest (H/M/L): how interested are they (likely to be) in the work?
  - Nature of interest: how do their interests intersect with the work, what are they likely to be most interested from the work?
  - Influence (H/M/L): how strongly might they be able to facilitate or block the work?
  - Comments on influence: why are they influential or not and how could they help or block the project?
  - (to be completed at end): Steps to engagement — if low interest and high influence, how should we engage with them and incentivise their attendance?

10.30 Stakeholder analysis
- As a facilitated group discussion, list stakeholders organisations and groups in column A (Mark to facilitate, someone to scribe)
- Look through prompts to identify missing stakeholders, including marginalised groups and those who typically work at different spatial scales e.g. international organisations

- Facilitated group discussion to describe each stakeholder, column by column (participants adding additional comments via post-it notes to ensure all knowledge is captured)

11.30 Break

11.45 Stakeholder analysis (continued)
- Individually complete the columns for all the remaining stakeholders, adding rows for additional stakeholders as they arise

13.00 Lunch

Plan A:

13:45 Checking the analysis
- All participants to check the work done by other participants, adding comments with post-it notes where there is 'disagree' or 'don't understand'
- Facilitated discussion of key points that people feel should be discussed as a group about stakeholders where there is particular disagreement or confusion and resolve these where possible (accepting differing views where it is not possible to resolve differences)

14.30 Next steps
- Identify 4–8 trusted individuals who you can check the analysis with, trying to get as wide a spread of different interests as possible (to do this, it may be necessary to start with a longer list and then identify people who are likely to provide similar views to reduce the length of the list)
- Identify stakeholders with high influence but low current engagement and ask:
  - What could motivate greater engagement?
  - What initial steps could we take to engage with them?

15.30 Close

Plan B (if stakeholder analysis not complete before lunch):

13.30 Stakeholder analysis (continued)
- Complete the matrix

14.30 Checking the analysis
- All participants to check the work done by other participants, adding comments with post-it notes where there is 'disagree' or 'don't understand'
- Facilitated discussion of key points that people feel should be discussed as a group about stakeholders where there is particular disagreement or confusion and resolve these where possible (accepting differing views where it is not possible to resolve differences)

15.00 Next steps
- Identify stakeholders with high influence but low current engagement and ask:
  - What could motivate greater engagement?
  - What initial steps could we take to engage with them?

16.00 Close

Materials
- Flip-chart paper
- Post-its
- OHP pens
- Marker pens
- Blu-Tack
- Pre-filled flip-chart paper
- Prompts to help identify stakeholders (photocopied to A3 if possible)
- A4 prompt sheet for facilitators showing common categories of stakeholder in case any have been omitted

Impact planning tool and example

1. Take a look at the example impact planning matrix over the page
2. Referring back to your stakeholder analysis, complete your own matrix for your research, starting with stakeholders who have most influence/interest first
3. In your own time, compile this into an impact plan with the following headings:
   a. Impact objectives
   b. Key messages (summarised from your impact planning matrix)
   c. Target audiences: your stakeholder analysis table, with stakeholders grouped into categories (e.g. patient groups, health professionals etc.) and listed in priority according to interest and influence
   d. Activities and resources: list activities chronologically from your impact planning matrix and identify the resources you will need to make these happen (this may include help from others and training). If you don't have the right resources, how might you adapt your activities or get the resources you need? Check the timings of activities with those who have responsibility for them and make sure that it aligns with your research plan
   e. Monitoring: Make sure each of your indicators is measurable and that you have the means to collect the data. Establish a means of monitoring your progress towards impacts e.g. an agenda item on a monthly project meeting, or by using an online impact tracking tool

Impact outcome or objective	Target stakeholders	Key messages	Delivery mechanism (KE activity)	Impact indicators (and means of measurement)	Risks	Risk mitigation	Responsibility and resources	Timing

257

Impact outcome or objective	Target stakeholders	Key messages	Delivery mechanism (KE activity)	Impact indicators (and means of measurement)	Risks	Risk mitigation	Responsibility and resourcing	Timing
Restore 20 million hectares of damaged peat bog by 2025, based on published research into the methods and benefits of restoration	• Ministers in Defra and devolved administrations • Environmental evidence analysts in Government departments • Government environment agencies	• 80% of UK peatlands are damaged and this has important costs to society • Damaged peatlands are making it harder to meet policy targets for climate, water & biodiversity • We have robust methods to restore bogs • Bog restoration can deliver climate, water & biodiversity policy goals	• Develop Peatland Code to publicly demonstrate progress towards policy statements on private-public partnerships for conservation • Policy brief • Presentations to policy analysts • Briefings to Ministers via trusted NGOs and other contacts • Input to development of Peatland Code	• Peatland Code developed, piloted & launched with high-level support from Government • Sponsorship funding levels (Peatland Code Register) • Number of hectares of land restored per year (Peatland Code Register)	• Change of Government to one opposed to Peatland Code • Change of Minister to one opposed to Code • Backlash from environmental NGOs opposed to carbon offsetting	• Launch Peatland Code before end of this parliament • Help civil servants develop effective Ministerial briefings • Develop a non-offsetting version of the Code for initial launch, from which NGOs can benefit before considering carbon markets	Mark Reed and Clifton Bain (IUCN) with support from IUCN team	2013-14: Inputs to develop Code 2014: Policy brief and presentations, briefings to Ministers November 2015: Peatland Code launch
	• UK based SMEs and multi-national corporations	• Peatlands are inspiring, iconic landscapes that are crucial to society • Bog restoration can tell a powerful story on the path to companies become carbon neutral • Peatland carbon is as cost-effective as woodland carbon but there are added benefits for water & wildlife and they last longer	• Develop Peatland Code to give guarantees to business sponsors that their money will deliver quantifiable carbon benefits • Short film • Brochure for sponsors about the Peatland Code • Catalogue of sponsorship opportunities • Brokerage and payment mechanisms	• Sponsorship funding levels (Peatland Code Register) • Number of hectares of land restored per year (Peatland Code Register)	• Lack of interest from businesses	• Commission market research	Mark Reed, Clifton Bain, James Byrne (Wildlife Trust), Chris Dean (Moors for the Future) and the Peatland Alliance (RSPB, National Trust and Wildlife Trusts) with support from consultant to help broker relationships with key businesses	2014

		• Targeted relationship & trust building with directors of sustainability from key businesses • Present at events and pitch to meetings with potential sponsors • Social media to raise awareness & get new leads & feedback					2013-14: Inputs to develop Code 2014: workshops with landowners
• Organisations representing landowners/managers	• Society is expecting more from peatlands and landowners need to be paid a fair price for work to restore and sustain their functions • The Peatland Code can complement public grants that only pay for initial restoration work by paying ongoing monitoring & maintenance costs over 30 years or more	• Relationship & trust building with key individuals & organisations • Workshops to explore risks & benefits with landowners • Short film • Information sheet for landowners • Input to development of Peatland Code • Identify land that can be restored under the Code	• Peatland Code developed, piloted & launched with broad support from land-owning community • Number of landowners benefiting from a fair price for restoration work (Peatland Code Register) • Number of hectares of land restored per year (Peatland Code Register)	Lack of interest from landowners	Engage representative organisations early in the process to help develop the Code Run workshops as soon as possible to get feedback from landowners and adapt the Code and our approach accordingly	Mark Reed and Kathleen Allen (PhD student) – funding required to finance travel and food/drink for workshops	

Social media strategy

1. Who/what are you promoting via social media?

Are you promoting your own personal research, a project or a group/institution?

2. Objectives

Describe your or your project/organisation's objectives for your social media plan using SMART (Specific, Measurable, Attainable, Relevant, and Timely) strategy.

Objective 1:	
Objective 2:	
Objective 3:	

Describe how these objectives support your planned impact goals, your project/organisation's mission, and how your organisation might be able to help you achieve your objectives:

3. Existing policies

Does your organisation have a social media policy, if so what does it include?

4. Audience

Who is likely to be interested in your research and who might use it? What aspects of your research are they most likely to be interested in, and how might they use your findings? Think of as many different groups or types of people and organisations as you can, and consider whether they will be interested in different aspects of your work. Use this to come up with a few different key messages from your work that these different audiences might be interested in:

Audience name	What do you want to happen as a result of engaging with them via social media?	Key messages you want to communicate to these audiences

5. Content Integration

Channel	Current Activity
Website	
Live Events	
Email	
Print	
Mainstream Media (TV, Radio etc.)	

To make life easier and keep a steady flow of material on your key messages, have a look at what you and your colleagues are already doing with traditional and other forms of digital media. Identify content that can be repurposed, remixed, or recycled for your social media strategy. Did you just integrate your findings into a conference talk or lecture? Can you put the slides online (e.g. via SlideShare)? Can you turn your speech notes or the class handout into a blog?

Identify content that can be repurposed, remixed, or recycled for your social media strategy.

6. Mavens, connectors and salespeople

To influence and achieve change, you need mavens, connectors and salespeople in your social network:

- **Mavens** are specialists in finding ideas and sharing facts with others, but tend not to interact with other users, mavens may be the first to share new results from a project.
- **Connectors** are master networkers; they tend to know a lot of people from different cultures and niches and are skilful at making contacts. For example, an effective connector may have contacts across different countries and continents with both social and environmental researchers, policy-makers and environmental managers, and with those that may not seem fully relevant to an idea or concept. The connector is often active over numerous social media platforms and as a result is the key individual for spreading idea epidemics and creating the kind of participation required for achieving social learning, when the connector shares information their reach is far and wide.
- **Salespeople** have skills (or powers) of persuasion. These are highly influential individuals, whose endorsement of new information can provide the level of trust in it required for people to believe it.

Think about what type of person you are, then identify people in your project/organisation who might complement your skills, who could work with you to implement a social media strategy for your project/organisation. Highlight those individuals who may play multiple roles.

Role	Individuals
Maven	
Connector	
Salesperson	

7. Tool Selection and Techniques

Can you repurpose material for use on multiple networks, for example, posting longer versions of key tweets as Facebook and LinkedIn posts? Bear in mind that there are different styles, conventions and types of content suited to different networks. Something with a slightly more personal edge might work well on Facebook, but everything needs to be strictly professional on LinkedIn. Pinterest and Instagram will need a powerful image (and this is also a major bonus for the Google+ interface)

Tool	Use
Twitter	
Facebook	
LinkedIn	

Blog	
Others	

8. Running a social media campaign

Think of a central activity around which you could build a social media campaign linked to your project/organisation/research (e.g. a new publication, event or call to action)

9. How could you make your social media content more creative and PUVV (personal, unexpected, visual and visceral)?

10. Do, Share, and Gain

Describe how you will build in elements of Do, Share and Gain into your plan. What do you want to get people who engage with your social media messages to do? What do you want them to share and what might make it attractive for them to do so? What will they gain personally from doing what you're asking them to do and sharing your message?

Tool	Use
Do	
Share	
Gain	

11. Evaluation and piloting

What metrics will you use to assess whether you are being successful or not? Do you want to measure this entirely in terms of interaction or can you also look at ways in which your engagement with social media is leading to measurable impacts on society? How will you use this data to improve your practice? Is there a small element of your plan that you can pilot with a particular audience? How will you collect and implement feedback?

12. Timeline and budget

Include a timeline for major tasks and identify whether you will need a budget to implement any part of your plan.

Further reading

Here are a few of my favourite texts on knowledge exchange and impact. Share yours with me at www.fasttrackimpact.com and I will update this list in future editions.

Books

Denicolo, P. (Ed.) (2013) *Achieving impact in research.* Sage.

Bastow, S., Dunleavy, P. and Tinkler, J. (2014) *The impact of the social sciences: How academics and their research make a difference.* Sage.

EU (2013) *Responsible Research and Innovation (RRI), Science and Technology: Summary.* Volume 401 of Special Eurobarometer, Publications Office, Brussels.

Nutley, S.M., Walter, I.C., Davies, H.T.O. (2007) *Using evidence: How research can inform public services.* Bristol: The Policy Press.

Prewitt, K., Schwandt, T.A., Straf, M.L. (2012) *Using science as evidence in public policy.* Washington, DC: National Academies Press.

Weiss, C.H., Bucuvalas, M.J., 1980. *Social Science Research and Decision-making.* Lexington, MA: Lexington Books.

Useful Articles

Albaek, E. (1995) Between knowledge and power: utilization of social science in public policy making. *Policy Science* 28: 79–100.

Berkes, F. (2009) Evolution of co-management: role of knowledge generation, bridging organizations and social learning. *Journal of Environmental Management* 90: 1692–1702.

Boaz, A., Fitzpatrick, S., Shaw, B. (2008) Assessing the impact of research on policy: a literature review. *Science and Public Policy* 36(4): 255–270.

Boaz, A., Locock, L., Ward, V. (2015) Whose evidence is it anyway? *Evidence and Policy* 11: 145–148.

Bornmann, L. (2012) Measuring the societal impact of research. *EMBO reports* 13: 673–676.

Contandriopoulos, D., Lemire, M., Denis, J.-L., Tremblay, E. (2010) Knowledge exchange processes in organizations and policy arenas: a narrative systematic review of the literature. *Milbank Quarterly* 88: 444–483.

Davies, H., Nutley, S., Walter, I. (2005) *Approaches to assessing the non-academic impact of social science research*. St Andrews: ESRC/Research Unit for Research Utilisation, University of St Andrews.

Fazey, I., Fazey, J.A., Fazey, D.M.A. (2005) Learning more effectively from experience. *Ecology & Society* 10: art 4.

Graham, I.D., Tetroe, J. (2008) Some theoretical underpinnings of knowledge translation. *Academic Emergency Medicine* 14: 936–941.

Grant, J., Hinrichs, S. (2015) *The nature, scale and beneficiaries of research impact: An initial analysis of the Research Excellence Framework (REF) 2014 impact case studies*. Higher Education Funding Council for England.

Greenhalgh, T., Fahy, N. (2015) Research impact in the community-based health sciences: an analysis of 162 case studies from the 2014 UK Research Excellence Framework. *BMC Medicine* 13: 232–244.

Hanney, S., Gonzalez-Block, M., Buxton, M., Kogan, M. The utilisation of health research in policy-making: concepts, examples and methods of assessment. *Health Research Policy & Systems* 1: 2.

Heaney, M.T. (2006) Brokering health policy: coalitions, parties, and interest group influence. *Journal of Health Politics, Policy & Law* 31: 887–944.

Holmes, J., Clark, R. (2008) Enhancing the use of science in environmental policy-making and regulation. *Environmental Science & Policy* 11: 702–711.

Kramer, D.M., Wells, R.P. (2005) Achieving buy-in: building networks to facilitate knowledge transfer. *Science Communication* 26: 428–444.

Landry, R., Amara, N., Lamari, M. (2001) Climbing the ladder of research utilization and evidence from social science research. *Science Communication* 22: 396–422.

Lavis, J.N., Oxman, A.D., Moynihan, R., Paulsen, E.J. (2008) Evidence-informed health policy 1— Synthesis of findings from a multi-method study of organizations that support the use of research evidence. *Implementation Science* 3: 7.

Legrand, T. (2012) Overseas and over here: policy transfer and evidence-based policy-making. *Policy Studies* 33: 329–348.

Oancea, A. Interpretations of research impact in seven disciplines. *European Educational Research Journal.* 2013: 12: 242–250.

Oliver, K., Innvaer, S., Lorenc, T., Woodman, J., Thomas, J. A systematic review of barriers to and facilitators of the use of evidence by policymakers. *BMC Health Serv Res.* 2014; 14: 2.

Owen, C., Hemmings, L., Brown, T., 2009. Lost in translation: maximizing handover effectiveness between paramedics and receiving staff in the emergency department. *Emerg. Med. Australasia* 21, 102e107.

Owen, R., Macnaghten, P. and Stilgoe, J., 2012. Responsible research and innovation: From science in society to science for society, with society. *Science and Public Policy* 39: 751–760.

Pardoe, S. Research impact unpacked? A social science agenda for critically analyzing the discourse of impact and informing practice. *SAGE Open.* 2014; 4:2.

267

Phillipson, J., Lowe, P., Proctor, A., Ruto, E. (2012) Stakeholder engagement and knowledge exchange in environmental research. *Journal of Environmental Management* 95: 56–65.

Ward, V., Smith, S.O., House, A., Hamer, S. (2012) Exploring knowledge exchange: a useful framework for practice and policy. *Social Science and Medicine* 74: 297–304.

Weiss, C.H., Murphy-Graham, E., Petrosino, A., Gandhi, A.G. (2008) The fairy godmother and her warts: making the dream of evidence-based policy come true. *American Journal of Evaluation* 29: 29–47.

By the author

Here are a few of my attempts to make contributions in this field so far. Although they have all been written in an environmental context (there are no journals dedicated to knowledge exchange, participation and impact), the insights from many of these papers are generalisable. You can find links to each paper on my website (www.profmarkreed.com). Contact me if you don't have access to any of the journals and I'll send you a copy.

de Vente, J., Reed, M.S., Stringer, L.C., Valente, S., Newig, J. (2016) How does the context and design of participatory decision-making processes affect their outcomes? Evidence from sustainable land management in global drylands. *Ecology & Society*

Reed, M.S. (in press) How social are social innovations? The role of social learning and deliberation in the emergence of social innovations. *Ecology & Society*

Reed, M.S., Curzon, R. (2015) Stakeholder mapping for the governance of biosecurity: a literature review. *Journal of Integrative Environmental Sciences* 12: 15–38.

Reed, M.S., Stringer, L.C., Fazey, I., Evely, A.C., Kruijsen, J. (2014). Five principles for the practice of knowledge exchange in environmental management. *Journal of Environmental Management* 146: 337–345.

Fazey, I., Bunse, L., Msika, J., Pinke, M., Preedy, K., Evely, A.C., Lambert, E., Hastings, E., Morris, S., Reed, M.S. (2014) Evaluating knowledge exchange in interdisciplinary and multi-stakeholder research. *Global Environmental Change* 25: 204–220.

Reed, M.S., Fazey, I., Stringer, L.C., Raymond, C.M., Akhtar-Schuster, M., Begni, G., Bigas, H., Brehm, S., Briggs, J., Bryce, R., Buckmaster, S., Chanda, R., Davies, J., Diez, E., Essahli, W., Evely, A., Geeson, N., Hartmann, I., Holden, J., Hubacek, K., Ioris, I., Kruger, B., Laureano, P., Phillipson, J., Prell, C., Quinn, C.H., Reeves, A.D., Seely, M., Thomas, R., van der Werff Ten Bosch, M.J., Vergunst, P., Wagner, L. (2013) Knowledge management for land degradation monitoring and assessment: an analysis of contemporary thinking. *Land Degradation & Development* 24: 307–322.

Reed, M.S., Bonn, A., Broad, K., Burgess, P., Fazey, I.R., Fraser, E.D.G., Hubacek, K., Nainggolan, D., Roberts, P., Quinn, C.H., Stringer, L.C., Thorpe, S., Walton, D.D., Ravera, F., Redpath, S. (2013) Participatory scenario development for environmental management: a methodological framework. *Journal of Environmental Management* 128: 345–362.

Fazey, I., Evely, A.C., Reed, M.S., Stringer, L.C., Kruijsen, J., White, P.C.L., Newsham, A., Jin, L., Cortazzi, M., Phillopson, J., Blackstock, K., Entwhistle, N., Sheate, W., Armstrong, F., Blackmore, C., Fazey, J., Ingram, J., Gregson, J., Lowe, P., Morton, S., Trevitt, C. (2012) Knowledge exchange: a research agenda for environmental management. *Environmental Conservation* 40: 19–36.

Prell, P., Reed, M.S., Racin, L., Hubacek, K. (2010) Competing structures, competing views: the role of formal and informal social structures in shaping stakeholder perceptions. *Ecology & Society* 15(4): 34.

Reed, M.S., Evely, A.C., Cundill, G., Fazey, I., Glass, J., Laing, A., Newig, J., Parrish, B., Prell, C., Raymond, C., Stringer, L.C. (2010) What is social learning? *Ecology & Society* 15 (4): r1.

Raymond, C.M., Fazey, I., Reed, M.S., Stringer, L.C., Robinson, G.M., Evely, A.C. (2010) Integrating local and scientific knowledge for environmental management: From products to processes. *Journal of Environmental Management* 91: 1766–1777.

Prell, C., Hubacek, K., Reed, M.S. (2009) Social network analysis and stakeholder analysis for natural resource management. *Society & Natural Resources* 22: 501–518.

Reed, M.S., Graves, A., Dandy, N., Posthumus, H., Hubacek, K., Morris, J., Prell, C., Quinn, C.H., Stringer, L.C. (2009) Who's in and why? Stakeholder analysis as a prerequisite for sustainable natural resource management. *Journal of Environmental Management* 90: 1933–1949.

Prell, C., Hubacek, K., Quinn, C., Reed M.S. (2008) 'Who's in the network?' When stakeholders influence data analysis. *Systemic Practice and Action Research* 21: 443–458.

Reed, M.S. (2008) Stakeholder participation for environmental management: a literature review. *Biological Conservation* 141: 2417–2431.

Prell, C., Hubacek, K., Reed, M.S., Burt, T.P., Holden, J., Jin, N., Quinn, C., Sendzimir, J., Termansen, M. (2007) If you have a hammer everything looks like a nail: 'traditional' versus participatory model building. *Interdisciplinary Science Reviews* 32: 1–20.

Reed, M.S., Dougill, A.J. ,Taylor, M.J. (2007) Integrating local and scientific knowledge for adaptation to land degradation: Kalahari rangeland management options. *Land Degradation & Development* 18: 249–268.

Fraser, E.D.G., Dougill, A.J., Mabee, W., Reed, M.S., McAlpine, P. (2006) Bottom Up and Top Down: Analysis of Participatory Processes for Sustainability Indicator Identification as a Pathway to Community Empowerment and Sustainable Environmental Management. *Journal of Environmental Management* 78: 114–127.

Dougill, A.J., Fraser, E.D.G., Holden, J., Hubacek, K., Prell, C., Reed, M.S., Stagl, S.T., Stringer, L.C. (2006) Learning from doing participatory rural research: Lessons from the Peak District National Park. *Journal of Agricultural Economics* 57: 259–275.

Stringer, L.C., Prell, C., Reed, M.S., Hubacek, K., Fraser, E.D.G., Dougill, A.J. (2006) Unpacking 'participation' in the adaptive management of socio-ecological systems: a critical review. *Ecology & Society* 11: 39

Acknowledgements

This book is based on research funded by the UK's Economic and Social Research Council (ESRC), Biotechnology and Biological Sciences Research Council (BBSRC) and the Natural Environment Research Council (NERC), with additional funding provided by the Scottish Government and the Department for Environment, Food and Rural Affairs (under the Rural Economy and Land Use programme and the Living With Environmental Change programme, LWEC) (the Sustainable Learning project), and the British Academy (the Involved project). I am indebted to the teams of researchers I worked with in both of these projects, in particular Ana Attlee, Ioan Fazey and Lindsay Stringer in the Sustainable Learning project, and Joris de Vente, Lindsay Stringer, Jens Newig and Sandra Valente in the Involved project. Thanks to Joanneke Kruisjen for valuable inputs to the thinking behind the key paper that emerged from the Sustainable Learning project. This book started life as LWEC's Knowledge Exchange Guidelines, and was then developed into a training manual I co-authored with Ana Attlee, to accompany the training course we developed together. Thanks to Susan Ballard (LWEC), Faith Culshaw (NERC), John Holmes (NERC/LWEC Fellow) and Barry Hague (editor) for their inputs to the LWEC KE Guidelines from which the principles in this book were derived.

Thanks to the knowledge exchange and impact experts who helped co-design the research that led to this book: Joanneke Kruisjen (School of Engineering, Robert Gordon University), Piran White (Environment Department, University of York), Andrew Newsham (School of African & Oriental Studies (SOAS)), University of London), Lixian Jin (School of Allied Health Sciences, de Montford University), Martin Cortazzi (Centre for Applied Linguistics, University of Warwick), Jeremy Phillipson (Department of Agriculture, Food and Rural Development, Newcastle University), Kirsty Blackstock (Social, Economic & Geographical Sciences, James Hutton Institute), Noel Entwistle (School of Education, University of Edinburgh), William Sheate (Centre for Environmental Policy, Imperial College London), Fiona Armstrong (Head of Knowledge Exchange, Economic and Social Research Council), Chris Blackmore (Open Systems Research Group, Faculty of Mathematics, Open University), John Fazey (Educationalist, Ty'n Y Caeau Consultants), Julie Ingram (Countryside and Community Research Institute, University of Gloucestershire), Jon Gregson (Institute of Development Studies), Philip Lowe (UK Research

271

Councils' Rural Economy and Land Use programme and Newcastle University), Sarah Morton (Centre for Research on Families and Relationships, University of Edinburgh) and Chris Trevitt (College of Law, Australian National University).

I am grateful to the following people who kindly gave their time to review and give feedback on early drafts of the book, and helped make it as useful as possible for as many readers as possible: Jenny Ames (Associate Dean (Research & Innovation) and Professor of Food and Nutritional Sciences in the Faculty of Health and Applied Sciences, University of the West of England), Gabriele Bammer (Professor, Research School of Population Health, College of Medicine, Biology and Environment, Australian National University), Mahantesh Biradar (Institute of Biomedical Sciences at Academia Sinica, Taipei, National Yang Ming University, Taiwan), Rebecca Colvin (PhD student, University of Queensland, Australia), Grant Campbell (PhD student, Cranfield University and James Hutton Institute), Georgina Cosma (Senior Lecturer in Computer Science, School of Science and Technology, Nottingham Trent University), Ged Hall (Innovation & Enterprise Senior Training and Development Officer, University of Leeds), Dr Ingrid Hanson (English literature scholar and author of William Morris and the Uses of Violence, 1856-1890), Steven Hill (Head of Research Policy, Higher Education Funding Council for England, HEFCE), Anne Liddon (Science Communications Manager, Newcastle University), Paul Manners (Director, UK National Co-ordinating Centre for Public Engagement), Catherine Manthorpe (Head of the Research Office, University of Hertfordshire), Rosmarie Katrine Neumann (PhD student, Newcastle University), Katharine Reibig (Researcher Development Policy Officer, University of Stirling), Elizabeth Stokoe (Professor of Social Interaction, Associate Dean for Research, School of Social, Political and Geographical Sciences, Loughborough University), and Steven Vella (PhD student, Birmingham City University and Newcastle University).

I am grateful to Ana Attlee for inspiring me to start on the journey that eventually led to this book while working as a post-doctoral researcher on the Sustainable Learning project, and for the subsequent contributions and feedback on drafts of our training manual, from which this book was developed. Thanks also to Ana for teaching me most of what I know about social media. Thanks to Clare Gately (my writing buddy), Megan Jamieson (my coach) and others from www.self-publishingschool.com for valuable feedback, encouragement and advice on navigating the Kindle store. Thanks to

Roz Taylor from Elevator UK for advising me on marketing and business strategy, and for empowering me to turn my fears into enthusiasm. Thanks to Rosmarie Katrin Neumann for drafting Chapter 20 and Sarah Buckmaster for research on HEFCE's impact case study database in Chapter 19. Thanks to Simon Maxell, Colin Smith, Catherine Duggan and Maggie Charnley from the UK Government's Department for Environment, Food & Rural Affairs (Defra) and Rosmarie Katrin Neumann for constructive feedback and edits on Chapter 19. Thanks to Emma Leech (Director of Marketing and Advancement at Loughborough University) for telling me about the problems associated with Advertising Value Equivalency and pointing me to CIPR resources. Some of the suggestions I've made in Chapters 14 and 15 are based on what I learned from training by Diana Pound from Dialogue Matters. Box 12 is based on questions designed by Ben Fuchs and Maggie Buxton from Cohesive ID. Questions 2 and 3 out of the eight questions to identify your impacts in Chapter 8 are adapted from the University of Leeds Impact Toolkit. Thanks to Steven Vella for inspiringly positive feedback on this book during the hard grind of writing up his PhD, and for inputs to various chapters (in particular Chapter 15 and advice on film-making). Thanks to Sarah Lyth for showing me where to get amazing copyright-free photography, to Joyce Reed for additional photography and formatting, and to Rosmarie Neumann for encouraging me to use more pictures. Thanks to everyone at Birmingham City University, in particular Hanifa Shah, for the creative freedom and inspirational leadership that has enabled me to chase my dreams. I wouldn't have been able to write any of this if it were not for Philip Lowe, Jeremy Philipson, Anne Liddon and the rest of the RELU family who gave me my first big break, some of the most terrifying early tastes of working with policy-makers, and the support and confidence I needed to pursue impact. Winning the RELU impact prize is still the proudest moment of my career. Thanks to Marianne Noble for proof reading the book. Finally, thanks to Madie Whittaker organising my life so I could write this book, and thanks to Joyce, my wife, for cutting through my wordiness and inspiring me every day to do what I can to make the world a better place.